The People
Burnopfield And
The Turnpike Road
Revisited

by

F.G. Newman
with the Sunniside Local History Society

Burnopfield Cricket Club fund raising.

Previous page: Jack & Lilian Uren, 18th November 1941.

Front cover: Jennie Brewis in the early part of the twentieth century. She later married Harold Potts and they lived at The Leazes. Jennie was a singer and member of the Operatic Society, and was described as being a born comedienne. She was also a member of the bowls club and Women's Institute. Jennie can be seen in later life on page 30, when the WI placed a seat next to the War Memorial in 1963.

Copyright © F.G. Newman & Sunniside Local History Society 2002

First published in 2002 by

The People's History Ltd
Suite 1, Byron House
Seaham Grange Business Park
Seaham
Co. Durham
SR7 0PY

ISBN 1 902527 91 7

Contents

While we were completing this book, very sadly, on 30th March 2002, Queen Elizabeth the Queen Mother died. We feel it appropriate to give a short summary of her family's historic relationship with the region.

In 1767 the marriage of Mary Eleanor Bowes of Streatlam and Gibside, heiress to the Bowes' estates in County Durham, to John Lyon, 9th Earl of Strathmore, merged the interests and estates of an ancient Durham family with those of an equally ancient Scottish house. For the ensuing 50 years the Earls of Strathmore identified themselves with their newly-acquired County Durham estates, an identification symbolised by their change of name from Lyon to Bowes. From 1820 to 1885 this close connection was severed and, although in the latter year the Earls of Strathmore re-acquired the estates, they were never again continuously resident in the county.

Elizabeth Bowes-Lyon (1900-2002) daughter of the 14th Earl of Strathmore married the Duke of York in 1923. On the abdication of Edward VIII in 1936, the Duke of York became King George VI. On the King's death in 1952 the Queen assumed the title of Queen Elizabeth the Queen Mother.

The Queen Mother maintained her ties with the region and returned frequently, she is featured on several pages in this book. Following a private visit to Gibside Chapel in 1964, she is pictured here on a further visit to Gibside in 1966 following the restoration of the Chapel.

Introduction

Our first two books *The Turnpike Road* and *Byermoor Marley Hill & Sunniside* were a resounding success, copies were sold in their thousands. We received letters of appreciation from all over the country and the world, from South Africa, New Zealand, Australia, America and Canada. Because of that there was always the temptation to produce another book but it was debatable whether or not we would.

It is thanks to the archives of the late Jack Uren that we are able to compile this third book. Jack was a respected former headmaster and local historian who lived at Burnopfield. When he died his son John used the archives to produce a book in his father's memory. John's book *Around Burnopfield* does justice to his father's memory, it is well written and an excellent record of the history of the area. We were indeed fortunate that John very generously passed on his father's archive material to us and gave us his permission to use them.

The archives touch on subjects from the Tyne to Durham City, especially, however, on the Burnopfield area and are a treasure trove, immense in volume and absorbing in content. With our own considerable archive material added to Jack Uren's we are able to embellish on the subject of Burnopfield and return once more to the Turnpike Road with new subjects and added information on those already covered.

It is not our intention to compete with John Uren's book, rather we would hope that this book will be viewed as an extension to *Around Burnopfield*. It will provide local history enthusiasts with a further detailed analysis of the history of our villages, Burnopfield, Byermoor, Marley Hill and Sunniside.

Burnopfield viewed from Crookbank.

Acknowledgements

I am very grateful to a number of people, primarily of course to the late Jack Uren, whose wonderful archive material was so necessary for the compilation and production of this book. I am equally grateful to Jack's son and daughter-in-law, John and Rosemary Uren who have been most generous with their help and contributions, even going so far as to travel from their home in Leeds with children John and Helen to deliver to me the entire contents of Jack Uren's archives. I am once more indebted to the contributors of our own archive material, including the detailed work of Peter Davison which continually comes into use, and to Thelma Nichols of Southend and Ruth Crossley of Lancashire for the Potts' contribution. I am grateful to Geoff Cook for his considerable help, including photographs, to add to the heroic story of his father James Arthur Cook. Also to Alma Willis of Swalwell Local History Society. For the support of my colleagues in our local history society and the assistance of society members Sheila McGahon, Joan Telford, Colin and Ethel Baker. Thanks once more to Margaret Newman for identifying photographs and most of all for putting up with my 'artistic temperament'.

Our appreciation goes once again to the officials and the committee of Sunniside Social Club for extending such wonderful facilities to the society. Not forgetting club stewardess Pauline and her staff for being so helpful and obliging.

Source of reference include:

Primarily the archives of Jack Uren

Around Burnopfield by John Uren
The Turnpike Road and *Sunniside, Marley Hill and Byermoor* by Sunniside History Society
The Old Halls of Durham by Neville Whittaker
The Bowes Railway by Colin E. Mountford
Durham Coal – A People's History by Andrew Clark & George Nairn
Polisses and Candymen by the Tommy Armstrong Memorial Trust
Tommy Armstrong Sings by Tom Gilfellon
The Chaldrons by John A. Elliott
Country Life a 1952 article by Christopher Hussey
The History of Gibside by James F. Robinson
Co-operation in West Stanley & District by John W. White and Robert Simpson
The Lang Village by Hylton Marrs

My thanks go especially to our friend Andrew Clark of The People's History for his expertise, guidance and hard work in producing this book.

We dedicate this book to the memory of
Jack and Lilian Uren

BURNOPFIELD AND TANFIELD

John Uren Jnr aged 3 years at the Queen
Elizabeth II Coronation party on the Cricket
Field at Burnopfield, 1953.

Looking from Byermoor Church on the A692, Burnopfield, half a mile ahead, appears to lie on a long narrow shelf, only a few hundred yards wide, between the high ground of Hobson and the steep slope into the Derwent Valley. Despite its now considerable size, Burnopfield originally only stretched the quarter mile from Busty Bank and Sheephill, to Bryan's Leap and the Fold, the oldest parts of the village. The old Lobley Hill Turnpike, on its way to Medomsley, was at that time the only road through.

Overlooking Grove Terrace from the Hobson Bank.

Coal always played a big part in the growth of Burnopfield. In 1960, the inscription 'J.H.1669' was found on a stone lintel above a fireplace in an old house in Bryan's Leap. These initials have been traced to a James Harrison, who was involved with the coal trade and thus we can assume that people have lived in the village for almost 400 years. To transport coal from the pits to the Tyne, narrow gauges were laid with two of these being carried by the world's first railway bridge, the nearby Causey Arch, built in the 1720s.

Although Burnopfield never had its own deep mine, people settled in Busty Bank and Bryan's Leap which were ideally positioned on the waggonways from Pontop Pike and Tanfield Moor. Soon, drivers of the horse-drawn waggons could quench their thirst at four public houses served by a brewery in Bryan's Leap and at two public houses with their brewery at Busty Bank. Nowadays, ironically, one which closed – the Grapes Inn – became a Methodist Manse in the 1890s and served as such until 1980.

Burnopfield is sprinkled with unusual place names. When a bankside on the hilly road to Rowlands Gill burst, exposing a coal seam, it was named 'Bursting Bank' and later 'Busty Bank'. The seam was named the 'Busty', and was worked in nearby mines. 'Bryan's Leap' probably came from a prodigious leap made on foot or horseback by someone of that name. Although one other theory is that it is a corruption of 'Bruins Leap'. Many years ago bear baiting was a common practice and maybe a bear being baited leaped into the dene to escape. Regardless of origin, for years Burnopfield was known as the 'Leap', or 'Loup' in local dialect.

A coal chaldron which has negotiated the waggonways to reach the Tyne.

The name Burnopfield is made up of Scandinavian and Saxon words. Burn is pure Saxon, and needs no explanation, as it is of course a small stream. The next part of the word is disguised for the sake of euphony (or easy pronunciation) – 'op' is a shortening of hope. Hope is a word of Norwegian origin, and was probably introduced into this country by the Vikings about the eighth century. It originally meant the place where one small stream met another one; but ultimately it came to mean the dene, or more properly, the head of the dene where it was narrowest. Field or Feld (Saxon or German) is somewhat different from our general acceptance of the term as an enclosure, and means properly an open space, and is the same as fell or moor. Burnopfield then is the fell or open country at the hope of the burn, and is perhaps properly the part of the village not far from the Burnopfield House. We find the same division as the last word in other places. For example Tanfield is a corruption of Teamfield – that is, the fell or field near Team River.

One other 'theory' concerns a band of marauding Scots who crossed the Tyne at Wylam in 1640 and routed an English force. Fleeing along the Derwent Valley and up the hill to a small hamlet with its fields of ripening corn, the English gave the order 'Burn Up Fields!' and escaped, hidden by the smoke!

The oldest house in the village, Burnopfield Hall, was built in 1720 by a wealthy coal owning family called Newton. In the late 1760s, Hannah Newton, heiress to the family fortune, met and married an Irish adventurer, Lieutenant Andrew Robinson Stoney, who was stationed in Newcastle. They went to live at Colepike Hall, Lanchester. There, his ill-treatment of her became a local scandal, and within a few years she died.

In 1746, John Wesley visited the scantily populated village and preached in a garden in Sheephill. Subsequent visits by him resulted in the formation of a Methodist Society and in 1775 the first chapel was built. It had an upper room above a stable where the itinerant preachers kept their horses during services. This room later served as a school. In 1880 the chapel was rebuilt on the same site. By this time, two other places of worship had been built: a second

Methodist Chapel in 1870 and, at the Leazes end of the village, the first Anglican Church in 1873.

From about 1870 development quickened. A school was built in 1872 and a big Co-operative Society Store in 1889. Burnopfield became a shopping centre for the mining families from the neighbouring colliery villages. 'Co-op' members were encouraged to save and buy homes in the newly built terraced houses.

For more than 100 years cricket has flourished in the village. It has produced two Test cricketers: Jim McConnon, of Glamorgan and England, and Colin Milburn, the 'Burnopfield Basher', who played for Northampton and England. Tragically, Colin's career was cut short by a car accident. Sadly, he died in 1990 and his funeral was the biggest ever seen in Burnopfield, being attended by cricketers from local to Test level, as well as his many friends.

In the past 50 years, Burnopfield has changed beyond all recognition from its old waggonway days. Most dramatic however, is the change in the occupation of its work force. With all the local mines closed, industrial estates, factories, offices and shops in the surrounding districts now offer employment to both men and women. New Council and private estates have been built; the village has extended east and west, absorbing most of the adjoining areas into its Postal District. Being within easy commuting distance of Newcastle with its magnificent views of the Derwent Valley.

Cricketer Jim McConnon.

Derwent View, leading to The Leazes, *circa* 1920.

The Hobson/Burnopfield Colliery

The following article was written in September 1903, the author unknown. It is interesting to note that the description he gives during his journey underground, varied little from the conditions which existed underground towards the closure of the colliery in 1968. There was one difference, it beggars belief that in those days miners were forced to work underground at the age of 70 years or more. One hopes that the greedy coal owners are still answering to a higher authority than that on earth, because clearly they answered to no one there.

The Hobson Pit with chaldrons in 1911.

The Hobson as it is commonly called, though Burnopfield Colliery is the correct title, is situated midway between Dipton and Marley Hill. It is an old colliery having been worked over half a century. The colliery is the property of Messrs John Bowes and Partners, the agent for whom is Mr Bartley of Marley Hill. Mr Benjamin Mason who is well known as a member of Lanchester Guardians, Tanfield District Council and School Board is the resident manager. The seams in which work is carried out are the Busty, Main Coal and Hutton; the Busty being the principal seam. 80 hewers are employed in that seam against only some 20 in the other 2 seams. The mine was singularly free from fire-damp and naked lights were used in every portion of the workings. The roofing for the greater part is excellent hence probably the rarity of accidents. The mine is lighted by electricity and there is also an electric pump in operation the cables for which extend a mile 'in by' (from the shaft to the face). I was privileged last Friday night through the courtesy of Mr Mason, the manager, to spend a few hours in the pit. Hours, which judging from the amount of sweat I lost, were not entirely fruitless from the training point of view.

Accompanied by a friend who's name is not altogether unknown in scholastic and football circles, I entered the cage about 6 o'clock and was swiftly conveyed to the Busty seam, a depth of 90 fathoms. Soon after our arrival there we were met by Mr Joseph Maddison, the master shifter, who kindly took us around his district; and an excellent and informing guide he proved. Prior to meeting Mr Maddison however, we had the pleasure of inspecting the stables in which were some very well fed horses and ponies. The horse keeper, whoever he is, apparently looks well to his work. Upon Mr Maddison's appearance upon the scene he invited us to accompany him to the furnace used for ventilating the mine and thither we journeyed travelling through a disused seam. The furnace man's brow and I should imagine the rest of his body was wet with sweat but he proclaimed to us that he felt in top condition.

Leaving the furnace, we travelled through the Jubilee district, which runs due east, travelling we were told to Crookgate bank and then in a southern direction towards Barcus Close. The roofing was good and there was no discomfort so far as the stooping process. This was to come. Leaving the straight path as one might term it, we journeyed to the face of the workings. At one point of our journey for a

A miner at the shaft bottom, *circa* 1890. Note there are no safety gates or rails. In those days safety was not a priority.

Miners at the end of their shift, *circa* 1920. There is no safety gate to prevent them falling as the cage moves, demonstrating again a total disregard for safety.

short distance the roof was but little over 2 feet in height and we scrambled through. Amongst the workmen was a Crimean War veteran, a warrior of 70 years of age who fought under Sir James Scarlett in the 5th Dragoon Guards. Mr Southern, was his name and he was present at the fall of Sebastapol in 1854. Our next visit was to a place in which deputies had just been engaged in drawing out timber,

The colliery winder house and coolant tanks.

thus practically closing the place in question from further operations. One or two hewers were seen engaged in their arduous labour and we then commenced our homeward journey. We again entered the cage but stepped out at the main coal seam for a few minutes.

There was a marked distinction between the temperature here and in the other seams. Here we bade goodnight to our guide and in a darkness that could be felt rode to bank and found awaiting us the best of all mining engagements, 'bait'. The Hobson air seems to tend to longevity. Mr Roger Mason, for many years manager of the colliery was 86 years of age on Friday last. Another, a veteran brakesman, Mr Thomas Brown, retired six months ago aged 76. Whilst there also survives, in the person of Mr Maddison Senior, one who was present at the sinking of the shaft half a century ago.

Burnopfield Colliery, *circa* 1960.

Waggonway and The Hobson Colliery

Following his partnership with William Hutt and his concern at what he regarded as an unstable company, George Bowes decided to investigate the coal lying under his own land. On his Gibside estate, some four miles south-west of Gateshead, lay the derelict Marley Hill Colliery. Coal was being mined here as early as 1665 but it had been abandoned by the Grand Allies as unprofitable in 1815, and about the same time the old waggonway which ran south-west from here to collieries at Burnopfield, Dipton and Pontop also became disused. So in the summer of 1839 Bowes formed the Marley Hill Coal Company, consisting of himself, Hutt (to whom Bowes lent the money needed as capital), Lady Strathmore (who took no active part in the firm's affairs) and Nicholas Wood, who was also the firm's engineer.

The sinking of the new colliery began in January 1840. The new pit lay quite close to the Brandling Junction Railway's Tanfield branch,

A section of the old Pontop to Burnopfield waggonway.

the famous waggonway built in 1727 which had been relaid as a railway and reopened in November 1839. It consisted almost entirely of rope-worked inclines, and Wood was the railway's engineer.

In 1844 steps were taken to reconnect the Hobson Pit at Burnopfield to Marley Hill on the initiative of the colliery's new owner, John Berkley of Newcastle. Work was begun in the autumn of 1844 and completed early in 1845. The biggest engineering work on this 21 mile line was the steep bank up to Burnopfield Colliery, known as Hobson Bank, for which a stationary engine proved necessary. The opening of this line also provided rail access to another colliery, Crookbank Colliery, about one mile south-west of Marley Hill, which was won in 1845, though its owners are unknown.

John Berkley also took in hand the rebuilding of the derelict waggonway which ran from the Hobson Pit on to Dipton. Work is said to have begun in 1842 but for some undiscovered reason was not completed. In December 1847 the Partners purchased Crookbank Colliery, whose owners had gone bankrupt, as did the unfortunate John Berkley, whose Burnopfield and Tanfield Moor Collieries were acquired in November 1849 (though Tanfield Moor was sold to James Joicey in September 1850). These additions meant that the firm now controlled both the Marley Hill-Burnopfield line and all three collieries on it, as well as the line from Kibblesworth to Jarrow with its collieries.

When the railway between Marley Hill and Burnopfield Colliery was reconstructed in 1844-45, the main problem was the steep bank, known as Hobson Bank, between Crookgate and Burnopfield. The line had to be cut out of and around the side of a hill on a ruling gradient of 1 in 25.3, and once again a stationary engine was found to be necessary. On a 1863 map the engine-house is shown on the north side of the line below Burnopfield Colliery, with a set of six sidings in front of it which may well have been worked by the engine. In later years this is said to have been a horizontal cylindered engine built by Black, Hawthorn & Co Ltd of Gateshead but, if so, it must have been the second engine here for Black, Hawthorn did not exist in 1844. About half way down the bank was a length of double track, which can only mean that it was possible to run a full and an empty set at the same time, as on the Black Fell incline. On each side of this section were curves of six chains radius, which would have needed large vertical rollers to accommodate the rope.

A locomotive climbing the Hobson Bank in 1945.

The inconvenience which an incline in the middle of two locomotive-worked sections totalling 414 miles would cause is obvious and so, in 1900, it was decided to allow locomotives to work over it subject to certain restrictions. Either then or not long afterwards the grade was altered to 1 in 35 with a short section of 1 in 20.6 near the top, and the bank made single line. Latterly the maximum permitted load was eighteen empties up and twenty loaded wagons down, with the brakes of at least two of the latter pinned down. In addition, before a train could leave Burnopfield Colliery its driver had to inform the crossing-keeper at Crookgate by telephone so that the crossing gates could be closed. The escape siding points altered for the main line and the signal protecting this siding pulled off.

The work involved in connecting a direct line between Pontop, Burnopfield and Marley Hill Collieries proved a resounding success and lasted until all of the coal mines were closed by 1968.

Hobson Crossing, 1968. The last locomotive to leave the pit.

The Waggonway End

Dipton Old Delight

John Bowes and Partners acquired 2,770 acres of the lower seams from the Pontop Pike lease. The company had been formed in 1846 and owned large mining interests in Northumberland and Durham. Their coal was shipped from the River Tyne to markets in the south and, in 1853, they built the Pontop and Jarrow Railway which served about thirteen collieries and drift mines along its length of fifteen miles. The Delight Pit at Dipton was the most western one, literally the end of the line.

In 1863 a proposed one mile extension to the summit of Pontop Pike (1,025 feet) was never realised. The Delight Pit was only developed in 1860 and when its potential was assessed in 1870 it still contained a lot of very good quality coking and gas coal with an estimated output of 300 tons per day, costing 3s 6d per ton to produce. The pit's disadvantage was its distance from Jarrow Staithes as the cost of transportation was 1s 6d per ton. At these costs the pit could make a profit of 10s per ton, but that could be increased to 12s 6d per ton if it was made into coke at the pithead. With this in mind the company built thirty four Bee Hive Coke Ovens on site. They also built forty six workmen's houses nearby for their workforce. After struggling for many years the colliery closed in 1909.

Shaft sunk in 1853, closed in 1909 – life of 56 years.

New Delight

With many geological faults causing the closure of the previous Delight Colliery, John Bowes and Partners sank another shaft to the Busty Seam and called it the 'New Delight'. It was situated $^3/_4$ mile to the east of the original. The estimate made in the 1870s regarding production at the new colliery was found to be a little too

optimistic. The Busty and the Brockwell seams were found to be heavily faulted and by the 1930s production was falling and costs rising. The problem was examined and it was concluded that even though there was plenty of good quality coal in the mine it was so badly faulted that the pit could not depend on 'machine working' and it would have to revert back to hand working. The resulting output was likely to be below what would be economic and although some of the short fall would be made up by reclaiming old pillars of coal it was unlikely that low costs would be achieved. The colliery finally closed down in 1940. With the closure of the Dipton Delight the Bowes Railway now terminated at Burnopfield Colliery.

Delight Shaft sunk in 1909, closed in 1940 – life of 31 years.
Workforce over the years: 1930: 44; 1940: 850.

Lintz Colliery

Lintz Colliery was first opened in 1855 by Messrs McClain and Prior and was continued by the former gentleman until 1885 when it was laid in. Several rows of miners' cottages were built and miners came from far and near seeking work and settled down in the new village. This village was in the area which had been given to the De Lynce family in the thirteenth century, and was surrounded by places named Lintz Green, Lintzford, Lintz Hall, and hence it was called Lintz Colliery. In 1889 it was re-opened by John Shield Esquire and it was working the main coal seam 3ft 3 inches thick at a depth of 20 fathoms. The Busty Seam, 8ft thick with a 2ft band of excellent fire clay in the centre, was 60 fathoms deep. The three quarter seam, 2ft 9ins thick, was 75 fathoms deep. Whilst sinking over the 40 fathom dyke, which many engineers believed to be a dipper, but which as the manager expected turned out to be a riser, coal was discovered. This dyke raised the seam to a considerable height from its proper level for about 200 yards and a strata which intervened under the riser, contained 3 seams of coal. The coal in this neighbourhood was peculiarly well adapted for coking as it was remarkably free from sulphur. The colliery was worked by two shafts: the Anna Pit and Billy Pit. They were about a quarter of

a mile from one another and between them had an annual output of about 83,700 tons, giving employment to about 260 men and boys. The pits finally closed in 1929. South Garesfield Colliery had already broken through to the workings and proceeded to still work the seams.

The Anna Pit, 1892.

When the pit was closed, the surface works were all cleared away. The shafts were filled up and the large pit spoil heaps were levelled. Today, there is practically nothing to show that mining flourished for hundreds of years in this district, except the grassed over sites of the old waggonways which in some cases are now pleasant country walks.

The Billy Pit, 1920.

Miners of the Anna Pit, *circa* 1900.

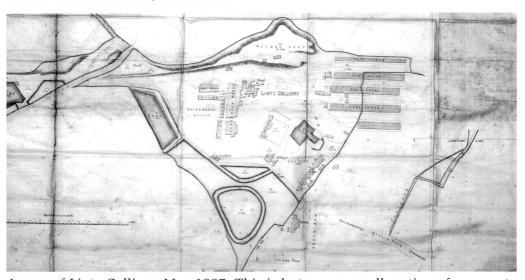

A map of Lintz Colliery, May 1887. This is but a very small section of a map at least 12 feet long and imprinted on a type of linen. It bears the words: 'Plan of part of the Lintz Estate belonging to the trustees of the late Richard Laycock Esq showing land damaged by Lintz Colliery Company May 1887.' It is signed by a Mr Dinning (Christian name illegible), Surveyor, Newcastle upon Tyne. The map is incredibly detailed and whilst in parts it looks hand drawn, there is no doubt that features are printed by machine. The coke ovens, colliery, school, housing, gardens and even the refuse heap are marked. Presumably it was originally intended to support a claim for damages by Richard Laycock against the Lintz Colliery Company.

The Lintz Mining Community

One of the streets was called School Street, even though the nearest school was half a mile away at Leazes. The building called the Miners' Institute, had originally been the village school, pupils paid a fee of twopence a week. Old school log books show that the Lintz Colliery School had opened on 20th July 1863, with a Mr Tait as its first headmaster. It was the first school in the area. This school was in operation for thirty-one years, and when it finally closed in 1894, its headmaster was Mr Richard Abbott who had held that position since 1887. Mr Abbott then opened the new Leazes Board School, and all the Lintz Colliery children moved there. In its early days the old Lintz school was occasionally used for Church of England Services. St James Church wasn't built until 1873.

The old school at Lintz then became a Miners' Institute, part of it being a dwelling house. The 'Tute', as it was affectionately called, had several billiards tables, and local boys spent a great deal of time playing there, even though money was hard to come by to pay for the games. To earn money they went around the village, shovelling miners' coals into their coalhouses for sixpence a load. The old institute boasted of a Lady English Snooker Champion, Ruth Harrison. Billiards' tournaments among the surrounding villages were a feature between the wars, and there were many excellent players. Snooker wasn't so common then.

The School and Institute. The institute was finally demolished with the old village, when the modern Council Estate was built.

Lintzford

Lintzford, as part of the Villa of Lintz, is very old and formed part of Lintz Green constabulary in Tanfield Chapelry. Finding records which deal with Lintzford alone has been difficult.

There is early mention of a road which led from the Lobley Hill Turnpike at Mountsett Bank which passed Low Ewehurst, Lofthouse and Lintz Hall and crossed the present Pont Burn Highway. Passing Lintz Green House, it continued down by the now disused Lintz Green Railway Station to Lintzford and then over the ford to join the highway on the other side of the Derwent Valley.

As the Villa of Lintz contained a large number of farms, it is feasible that some effort would be made to provide the means for grinding corn, probably by hand in the first instance but later by water power. A corn mill was certainly built at Lintzford but at what exact date is not recorded, although documents available do indicate that there was definitely a mill of some type at Lintzford prior to 1578.

Lintzford was really a part of Rowlands Gill although it is historically older and as its name implies, there was once a ford there over the river. In 1694 the

The Lintzford Mill.

corn mill was let by Christopher Hunt to John Sandford, the rent being £7 and 'one sword blade well made and tempered'. In 1703 Sandford converted the corn mill into a paper mill, Mr George Pearson was the next tenant of the paper mill. In 1712, Thomas Wetherby of Leadgate and Thomas Badge of Armonside were the new tenants, with a rise in rent to £10 per annum plus sword blade, a further tenant was Isaac Gilner. In 1780 the Annandales of Shotley Bridge took over the factory and ran it as a paper mill until 1912. They built Lintzford House in 1790, though later during some alterations to a bedroom in the house, a beautiful example of dragon wing roofing was discovered which points rather to an earlier period. The house was listed as an ancient monument.

Right: Lintzford House.

Charles Marsden took over and ran the paper mill until 1922. Richardson Printing Ink Company then took over and in 1923 converted the mill to suit their purposes, they employed 60 workers. They also inherited deeds written on parchment complete with huge wax seals and some written in Latin for the corn mill and land dated 1695.

In 1966 the firm was taken over by Due Faith Paints Limited but was still known by its former name. There was a small village of about 20 houses which were demolished in 1966. In 1990 the prominent tall stone chimney was demolished and the buildings were converted into up market housing.

Right: The Ink Factory.

Below: The Old Village.

The Co-op

The old Burnopfield Co-op, 1889.

It is over 157 years since the 'Rochdale Pioneers' founded the Co-operative Movement in 1844. The Burnopfield Society was one of many.

The Burnopfield Co-operative Society was formed as a breakaway from the Blaydon Co-operative Society on 25th May in 1889 when the society was established as an independent society. A committee and a general manager were all appointed on 8th June, and the society came into being on 18th September with grocery, butchery drapery, millinery and footwear businesses, together with a hall. Education activities, including a reading room and library, were also placed in the hands of a general committee, and several domestic properties were also acquired.

Poor economic conditions in the 1890s led to some staff being 'made idle', and in 1892 £50 was granted for relief of those in need and CWS aid was distributed to local schools. However, a new branch of the Burnopfield Co-op was opened in Hookergate selling groceries and footwear. In the village, greengrocery and tailoring departments were opened and, for a short while, there was a dressmaking department too. House building, however, was a prime objective, with 17 built in 1894 and, in 1900, 13 houses were completed in Hookergate. These were awarded to members applying for houses by ballot.

Temperance was not apparently prevalent, given the defeat of a motion by 28 votes to 21 'that in future no members under the influence of intoxicating drink be admitted to any meeting in connection with the Society.' Two other branches were also opened in Rowlands Gill and Sunniside. In addition to the three branches, there were travelling vans in butchery, greengrocery and hardware and a mobile bread van for a time. The society slaughtered its own cattle and, as early as 1912, hired out its hall for the showing of films. When the general manager resigned in 1913 for reasons unknown, there were 193 applications for the vacant post.

Dividends depended on turnover, which in good years exceeded £100,000 with a dividend of 4s 2d in the pound (21p) reached in 1907. After a period of strong years during the war, with the Durham coalfield just off its 1913 peak production, sales fell in the slump of the 1920s from £282,000 in 1920 to £138,000 by 1930. A funeral furnishing service opened at this time, with new branches at Highfield and Hobson. Periods of optimism were balanced by disappointment, and many developments, such as the retail of coal, were short term. Milk distribution came and went, and a drug department opened at Rowlands Gill in 1941.

The post-war period was a time of expansion with new grocery branches at Crookgate Bank Top and Leazes and a butchery at Rowlands Gill. Chemists businesses opened in Burnopfield and Sunniside, and travel, chiropody and catering were established, and the first self service store opened in Highfield in 1959. More stores converted, and a new filling station was acquired, which held an agency for Hillman Cars, later part of the Rootes group.

The late sixties was a difficult period owing to pit closures in the area, and the society eventually amalgamated with the Craghead and Holmside, Swalwell and West Stanley Societies to form Towneley on 12th October 1969.

Many changes took place over the years but the days of the Co-op were numbered and closure took place in January 1985.

Where once the mighty Co-op stood a variety of shops trade, a SPAR, butchers, chemists, fish & chip shop and an Italian pizza parlour. The adjoining building, the Grand Cinema which was so important to the entire community years ago, is now transformed into shopping units.

The Co-op's last day, 12th January 1985.

Major renovations to the Grand Cinema in 1990 – the first of many changes.

Right: The Grand Cinema converted to shop units, 2002.

The St John Ambulance Brigade Burnopfield Division, 1907-73

In the year 1903, a number of men of the village of Burnopfield decided to start a first aid movement. They enlisted the aid of Dr H.W. Boland and he agreed to help. He assisted by holding meetings in his home. In 1907, they were registered as a Division in the St John Ambulance Brigade and Mr W. Goodenough was elected Superintendent.

The Division officially enrolled on 16th February 1907. Superintendent Mr W. Goodenough is seated fourth from the left.

At this stage it was decided to branch out further and that the Division enlist the aid of a few prominent local men with a view to raising enough money to build an ambulance station and purchase an ambulance van. So a committee was formed under the chairmanship of Mr W. Braidford Jnr. Plans were drawn up and passed by the local council and the contract to build the station was given to local builders A.&R. Davis, the estimate being £200. The ambulance van was to be made by Sir W. Angus of Newcastle at a cost of £100. The men of the Division and the committee worked hard collecting one penny per week going from door-to-door in Burnopfield and District. Miners from local collieries had a penny per week deducted from their wages. Coal owners contributed as did the local council. Mrs Watson of Burnopfield House generously donated land on which to build the station and work commenced.

On 14th August 1909, the new station was opened by Miss Mabel Watson with the Chairman Mr W. Braidford Jnr presiding. Also present included: Miss Surtees of Hamstereley; Lieutenant C.B. Palmer, Assistant Commissioner of St John Association; Dr H.W. Boland, Honorary Surgeon of the Division; and Father Wilson of Byermoor.

The new station consisted of a lecture room and an ambulance house, to garage the ambulance van. When the van was in use, a horse had to be borrowed from the local Co-op or from the local collieries. Nursing utensils for use in the home were available to the public free on the production of a doctor's note.

The 1909 Ambulance Parade passing Grove Terrace.

The Division was organised with great precision and many people were involved, a list of trustees consisting of six people was drawn up, an Administration Committee of eighteen people was formed, as was an Ambulance Van Committee of eleven people.

On the outbreak of the First World War, inevitably Divisional members were called up, with resultant casualties. Three members lost their lives: Mr J. Macriesh, Mr J. Brennan and Mr M.J. Hines. Yet a further committee was formed to give a welcome home to the survivors and provide a Roll of Honour for all the members who took part in the First World War. In 1920, the Roll of Honour was unveiled in the station by Major Waring MP.

Residue from this fund was given to the Division to help buy a new motor ambulance van. Money was also contributed toward the building of a war memorial in the village to honour all who died from Burnopfield and District.

Burnopfield Ambulance Station.

Some members of the 1968 Brigade.

Every Armistice Day the Division paraded to a service at the Leazes Church and then to the cenotaph where they laid a wreath of poppies.

For many years, the Ambulance Division and the Ambulance Van Association worked together. Then the Division became a separate body but with the Division still having representation on the Van Committee. In 1948, the National Health Scheme was developed and Durham County Council took over the ambulance van and driver. When the van was sold to the County, the money was handed over to the Division for improvements to the ambulance station but the trustees were still responsible for the station.

It was impossible to extend the station on the ground so the decision was taken to build upwards. This was carried out and on 26th September 1953 the extension was opened by County Commissioner Sir Myers Wayman accompanied by Lady Wayman, County Superintendent Nursing, assisted by Mr C.R. Hall, President of the Trustees. Many other dignitaries attended as well as a large number of the community.

Throughout the years the Division had been well supported by the members of the Ladies Committee who had worked to raise money for uniforms and the upkeep of the building.

The Ambulance Cadet Division was started and registered as a Division on 29th June 1954 and Mr W. McKie was elected Superintendent.

A Nursing Division was formed in 1959 with Mrs E. Tinnion as Superintendent. This was followed by the formation of a Nursing Cadet Division with Mrs J. Taylor as Superintendent.

In 1965 Dr Stephen Boland, son of Dr H.W. Boland the founder of the Division, was presented with a wallet full of notes by Mr C.H. Metcalfe. A gift from the residents of Burnopfield on his retirement as a doctor in the village where he had served for 31 years. His father before him had been in the village 40 years as doctor.

The Ambulance Cadet Division started and registered on 29th June 1954 with Mr W. McKie (on the left) as its Superintendent.

St John Nurses (formed in 1959) with Mr C. Caisley (Superintendent, 1959-65) seated on the right. Edna Tinnion, the Nursing Division Superintendent, is seated next to him.

Superintendents through the years

1907-13	Mr W. Goodenough	1913-31	Mr R.J. Nesbitt
1931-33	Mr W. Kay	1933-37	Mr J. Swainston
1938-44	Mr A. Watcham	1945-46	Rev W. Southern
1947-48	Mr J. Burn	1949-52	Mr J.T. Liddel
1952-59	Mr T. Hugle	1959-65	Mr C.W. Caisley
1966-71	Mr C.H. Metcalfe	1971-73	Mr R. Thompson

The St John Ambulance, Burnopfield Roll of Honour:

2nd Lieutenant F. Braidford, Royal Northumberland Fusiliers
Quarter Master Sergeant R.J. Nesbitt Royal Army Medical Corp

Sergeant D. Clark RAMC

Sergeant U. Davison RAMC

Sergeant J. Treglowan DCM RAMC

Corporal J. Amis NF

W.C. Bone RAMC

G. Eltringham RAMC

J.W. Hall RAMC

F. Kendal RAMC

W. Ridley RAMC

J.A. Sinclair RAMC

T. Trewick RAMC

Privates: W.S. Armstrong RND, R.A. Bone RNF, S. Bateman RAMC, J. Blackmore RAMC, J. Bateman RAMC, W.A. Arnold RAMC, J.W. Pinkney, F. Patterson, J. Smitham, W. Smitham, J.J. Taskas, N. Wailes, J. Batey, W. Brown, P. Cairns, J. Dunphy, R. Ellis, W. Ellis, S. Elliott, L. Hilley, J. Jennings, T. King, J.T. Liddel, S. Murray, R. Nichols, J. Nichols, all of the RAMC. As well as J.W. Spurr RAMC, J.J. Scorey RAMC, J. McCann RND, W. Scorey Royal Military Field Ambulance.

The names of those killed in action:

Private J. Brennan Northumberland Fusiliers, J. McCreash Royal Engineers, J. Hines DLI, T. Burns RAMC, died as a prisoner of war in Japan 1943.

The Corps was disbanded in 1973.

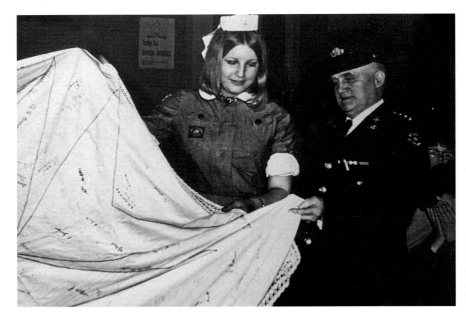

Charles Metcalf and Nurse D. Coxon.

The Burnopfield & District War Memorial

Horseguards is where we always meet
Ten thousand pairs of trudging feet
Assembling there in cold November
Just to prove we still remember
'Lest we forget' the epitaph
That draws us to the cenotaph.
The ghosts of an army of slaughtered souls
Are there with us as the drum rolls
'Come back Peter, come back Paul'
Said the childhood rhyme on the nursery
wall.
But Peter and Paul, with a million more
Never came back from that bloody war.

The cenotaph is dedicated primarily to those members of the Armed Services who gave their lives during the two world wars, although there has been names added since its unveiling.

The public raised the necessary finance and on 29th January 1921 the community assembled at the Temperance Hall and marched to the memorial. The Chairman of Tanfield UDC, Councillor J. Trotter officially unveiled the memorial.

The cenotaph at Burnopfield.

The base of the cenotaph.

The memorial is greatly valued by the community as this photograph of the 1976 Armistice Parade testifies.

In November 1963 the Women's Institute placed a seat next to the memorial, no doubt for members of the community to rest or sit in quiet contemplation. Unfortunately the seat is no longer there.

Corporal James Arthur Cook MM

Many brave men from the area gave their lives during conflict, some above and beyond the call of duty. There were those who committed great acts of bravery and received awards of the highest honour, one such man was Corporal James Arthur Cook No 300555 of the 8th Battalion Durham Light Infantry. James received the Military Medal by order of General Sir H.S. Rawlinson, Bart, GCVO, KCB, KCMG commanding Fourth Army during the First World War, on 17th June 1918. During active service in France he was a member of the Signal Unit in the DLI when enemy fire severed the overhead lines and communications were broken. James clambered up a telegraph pole and, even though under fire, he succeeded in repairing the lines and restoring vital communications. He went on to be promoted to sergeant.

James Arthur Cook.

We are fortunate in having a photograph of his campaign medals including the Military Medal 'For Bravery In The Field'. (*Left.*)

After the war James returned home and at the Holy Trinity Church in Pelton on 7th June 1923 he married Annie Spry, a Pelton Fell girl. They lived at Byermoor and had two children, Geoff and Muriel. Sadly Muriel died at an early age. James was an electrical engineer for Byermoor and Marley Hill Collieries and went on once again to serve his country during the Second World War by joining the Home Guard. He was awarded the rank of lieutenant.

James died in 1948 and because the family lived in a colliery house they had to arrange alternative accommodation. Geoff was due to commence his National Service that year and following his 'demob' from the Army he and his mother bought a cottage in Burnopfield.

Left: James and Annie on their wedding day.

Churches

The history of the churches and chapels in the Burnopfield area has been well documented, especially in John Uren's fine book *Around Burnopfield*. I feel, however, that the history of the Hobson Methodist Church, which played such an important part in the lives of the community, is worthy of a more detailed look.

The First Chapel

The building of the first chapel in 1859 was a memorable event, voluntary workers hewing the stones out of a quarry nearby. The chapel cost £142, and the total debt when it was opened was £40. This sum was borrowed from Andrew Hindmarsh of Burnopfield but in less than ten years it had been paid off and the chapel was free from debt. The building had a seating accommodation for 140 adults.

In 1868 Stanley was made a separate circuit, and in 1884 White-le-Head circuit was formed from Stanley. The new circuit was composed of societies at White-le-Head, Dipton, Marley Hill, Causey Row, Burnopfield Colliery, High Spen, Hamsterley Colliery and Victoria Garesfield. The total membership of these eight societies was 371 full members. The circuit was served by twenty-five local preachers, and there were twenty-seven class leaders. The minister lived at White-le-Head, but a few years later came to live at Burnopfield, and for reasons of convenience the name of the circuit was changed to Burnopfield.

Expansion

In 1884, when the new circuit was formed, there were thirty-six members at Hobson. During that year the Circuit Quarterly Meeting, under the chairmanship of the Rev Matthew Johnson, gave the trustees permission to secure a site for the erection of a new chapel. The site, costing £35, was purchased from the Ecclesiastical Commissioners, and conveyed to the trustees on the 31st December 1890. The Primitive Methodists at Burnopfield Colliery secured a site by the side of the west of the village and plans were prepared by architects, Messrs Davidson and Bendle, of Grainger Street, Newcastle. The foundation stones of the new chapel were laid in 1890. The chapel was capable of seating 250 adults, and at the rear was a large vestry which could be opened into the main building by folding doors. The work was carried out by Messrs A. & R. Davis, Burnopfield, masons, and Mr W. Maughan, of Lemington, joiner. The opening services were held on Saturday, 16th May 1891, when the Rev J. Hallam, President of the Conference, preached to a large company in the

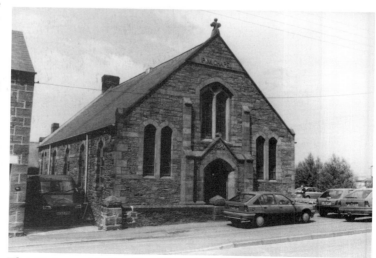

The Hobson Methodist Church.

afternoon. A meeting was held in the evening, presided over by Mr T. Brabban, of Marley Hill, Mr J. W. Bell, secretary to the Chapel Trust, read a report, showing that the chapel had cost £750, towards which £400 had been raised. The total cost of the chapel, including the purchase of the land, legal expenses, architect's commission, heating apparatus, harmonium, furnishings and other expenses, came to £830. Towards this amount £193 had been transferred from the old Chapel Trust Account, and the building was opened for worship on Whit-Saturday, 16th May 1891.

The Sunday School

It is not known when the Sunday School was commenced, but it must have been soon after the opening of the first chapel in 1859. It had always been an important department in the life of the church. In those days Sunday School Anniversaries were held out-of-doors in a marquee because the chapel accommodation was inadequate.

In 1907 a site at the rear of the church was purchased from the Ecclesiastical Commissioners for the erection of a Sunday School building. Many years passed, however, before the foundation stones were laid. This great event took place on Saturday, 9th December 1933. Memorial stones costing £5 were laid by past and present members of the church. The Sunday School was opened on Saturday, 21st April 1934, by Mr J. Underwood of Bishop Auckland. The Rev W. Atkinson presided. After the opening ceremony a short service was held in the church, the preacher being the Rev J. B. Moore. The building consisted of a schoolroom, with accommodation for 250 adults or 300 children, and a vestry capable of seating sixty adults. It cost £1,361, but furnishings and sundry expenses brought the total cost to £1,531.

Methodist Union was consummated in September 1932, and in 1935, the Burnopfield circuit, after fifty-one years of autonomy, became part of a large circuit consisting of forty-three churches and known as the Gateshead West Circuit. The Rev Samuel Palmer was the superintendent minister, and the Rev John T. Goodacre was in charge of the local churches. In 1938 the Gateshead West Circuit was divided and Hobson was attached to a new circuit consisting of seventeen churches called the Gateshead South Circuit. The Reverend George Fawcett was the first superintendent of this circuit.

The church remained at the centre of the community for many years. It was also attended by people from nearby Burnopfield and indeed some of the farther flung villages. However, like all communities, following the closure of the coal mines the number of inhabitants began to dwindle, as a consequence the church congregation became less and less. Eventually the decision was taken to close the church as a place of worship and on Sunday 22nd September 1974, on what must have been a very sad occasion, the last service was held. The building is now used by a local company as a showroom.

Reverend & Mrs J.P. Ellis, minister during the World War years – 1939 to 1946

Burnopfield Floral, Horticultural and Agricultural Society

The Burnopfield Show was a popular venue over many years. Crowds came from all the nearby villages to enjoy a family day out. There was all kinds of events arranged with a view to entertaining adults and children alike. The following details, extracted from the Diamond Jubilee celebrations, gives a fascinating insight into just how much effort and planning went into the society and how many people were involved.

The Diamond Jubilee Show, 1873-1933

The Show will be opened at 2 pm on Saturday August 19th, by Sir Arthur Lambert Kt, MC, JP and Lady Lambert of Newcastle upon Tyne.

In 1873 it was first suggested to have a Flower Show at Burnopfield, by Mr Twizell, gardener to Miss Surtees, of Hamsterley Hall.

A meeting was called for the purpose of commencing a show, and held at the house of Mr Adamson, the Black Horse Inn. At the meeting it was decided to hold a show, and the officials and committee were selected.

The first president was W.R. Dickinson, of Derwent Cote with the following as vice-presidents: Hodgson Hind MP, Viscount Gort, Lady Gort, Miss Surtees, of Hamsterley Hall, W.M. Annandale, G.H. Gooch, Jas Annandale, F. Priestman, Wm Braidford Snr, W.M. Handcock, Jas Turnbull, W. Addison, W.J. Handcock, J. Charlton and J. Robinson.

The society was well supported by the president and vice-presidents, with a strong committee. The first officials being: chairman and treasurer; Mr Thos Smith. Secretary: Mr Jas Hood, Lintz Green.

The highland dance team proved to be a major attraction and typical of the diverse activities.

After a year or two, Mr Thos Watson, tailor, of Burnopfield, was chosen as chairman, with Mr Dawson as vice-chairman, Mr W.M. Handcock as treasurer, and Mr Hood holding the position of secretary. The committee chosen being Messrs G. Davis, B. Mason, G. Gray, J. Burnip, W. Hunter, W. Hogarth, H. Charlton, J. Smith, J. Rowell, W. Rowell, D. Kirkup, J. Watson, B. Cowan, J. Davidson, gardener to Gibside Estate, and J. Twizell, gardener, Hamsterley Hall.

The first show was held in 1873, in the field, close to Crookgate. The band to play at the first show was Winlaton Band.

All the above-mentioned gentlemen took a keen interest in the society, and were very successful in the exhibits which they produced, most of these were considered of no mean order. The society has been the means of encouraging many amateur gardeners.

During the 60 years, the society has had four presidents, the late W.R. Dickinson, Derwent Cote; Wm Annandale, Lintzford; W.H. Bulman, late of Priestfield House, and the present president, Col F.R.A. Shiel, DSO, Leazes Hall, who has been president since 1919 and who takes a great interest in the society.

There have been five chairmen: Messrs Thos Smith, Thos Watson, W. Dawson, G. Humble, and the present chairman, Mr R. Abbott, who has held the position for 20 years, and has been connected with the society for 45 years. There have been four vice-chairmen: Messrs W. Dawson, G. Davis, R. Heslop and R. Hodgson who now holds the position, has been connected with the society for 20 years.

There have been three treasurers: Messrs T. Smith, W.M. Handcock (who was a great exhibitor and gained many prizes) and W. Braidford, who has now held the position for 15 years, and has been connected with the society for 45 years. There have been four secretaries. The first was Mr Jas Hood, Lintz Green, who was succeeded by Mr B. Mason, of Hobson; then Jas Weedy, and the present secretary, J. Marshall, who has held the position for 29 years, and been connected with the society for 35 years. The financial secretary, assistant secretaries, and the majority of the committee have been connected with the society for 20 years.

The society committee. By its volume demonstrates the number of activists required to organise and run the society.

Village Schools

by Jack Uren

I wonder how many of the older people who read this, remember learning to write at school using a slate and a squeaky slate pencil. Pens, dipped in the ink-well, and exercise books came much later. I started Leazes School in 1913 and that is how my education began. At least three quarters of the children came from mining families. Times were hard, but on the whole, happy. Members of the staff were: headmaster Mr Dick Abbott (he had quite a reputation), Mrs Hogarth (I don't think anyone ever knew her first name), Mr Bob Handcock, Miss Maggie Aynsley, Miss Blanche Holmes (Blanche Terrace, Tantobie is named after her) and Mr Jimmy Greenacre. These were the permanent members of the staff, others came and went.

Leazes School, like the schools at Burnopfield and Pickering Nook, catered for children from the age of five to fourteen. Emphasis was placed on Reading, Writing and Arithmetic. After morning assembly the day usually began with mental arithmetic, and from every classroom came the sound of 'Twice one are two, twice two are four' and so on. Knowledge of 'Tables' was a must, no calculators then. Other subjects taught were History and Geography, chiefly about the British Empire. Music – my remembrance of this is standing with the rest of the class in front of a Modulator (I think that is what it was called) with musical scales printed on it, and singing up and down the scale with gusto. Physical Training – it was called Drill then – consisted chiefly of standing in the aisles between the desks doing 'arms bend, knees stretch' exercises. Practical subjects like Domestic Science, Woodwork and Science were unheard of.

Children normally left at fourteen, but there was a scheme whereby a child could leave at the age of twelve and take up work. If the parents wished, their

A Leazes School class with headmaster Dick Abbott, *circa* 1910.

children could sit what was then called a 'Labour Examination' at the age of twelve, and if they satisfied the examiners that they had reached a sufficiently high standard in the 'Three R's', they could leave and take up work. Family income was so limited in those days that many parents took advantage of the scheme so that their children could start earning at an earlier age.

The boys usually went to work in the neighbouring mines, and many of the girls went 'to Place', in other words to Domestic Service, where they were 'Placed' to work in some well-to-do person's house.

About 1911 Tanfield Higher Elementary School was built, and this later became a Secondary School re-named Alderman Wood School after Alderman Curry Wood who lived in Burnopfield. Children then, at the local Board schools, had the opportunity of taking an entrance examination for admission to this school. This examination was rather fearsome for the youngsters of eleven-plus in those days.

It consisted of two written examinations followed by a personal interview. Many children did not do themselves justice and failed because of their nerves. This type of examination was eventually abandoned.

Leazes School opened in 1894 and continued until 1968, it then closed to be used as the Burnopfield Community Centre.

The first mention of education in the Burnopfield area is in 1730 when a rent charge of £6 per year was devised by Robert Robinson of Bryan's Leap for the education of children in the chapelry. Methodist preacher William Hopper conducted a day school at Sheep Hill over his horse's stable between 1746 - 1748. It is possible that the school remained in service until around 1870.

Around that time the United Methodist Chapel, The Grove, opened and a Sunday School room underneath the chapel was used as a Day School. There was a succession of teachers among them Obadiah Dickinson (1828), John Dodd (1851) and George Todd (1856). On the opening of the Grove Methodist School Mr Maddison went there from the National School in 1879. Mr Ward the schoolmaster was followed by Mr McAndrews and finally Mr G.H. Smith who left there in 1893 to go to Pickering Nook School.

There were also the Lintz Colliery School (1863-93), replaced by the Leazes Board School (1894-1968), the Masonic Lodge School, formerly the National School (1872-1968) and Pickering Nook School (1892-1982).

Burnopfield Secondary Modern School opened in 1933 under headmaster Mr Edward Bell, who was followed by Mr Mackerell. Mr Jack Uren became headmaster in 1956 and during a re-organisation in 1968, he and the children transferred to Shield Row Secondary Modern School

Burnopfield Secondary Modern School building became Burnopfield Junior and Infants' School, taking all the children from the National School and the Leazes Board School. Mr Beckham, the headmaster of Leazes Board School, became headmaster of the new school. In 1976, a new building was opened and the school was divided into separate junior and infants' schools. It is now Burnopfield Primary School and Nursery.

A Grove School class, *circa* 1890.

Burnopfield Junior School, *circa* 1910.

Four teachers welcome pupils on the first day of the new school year at Burnopfield Secondary School in 1933. Left to right: J. Freek, R. Whaling, N. Hopper and H. Buglass.

Burnopfield Modern School staff in 1955. Jack Uren is seated second from the left.

Shield Row staff, 1971. Back row: H. Cockleton, J. Hall, L. Graham, Mr Lyth, T. Stokel and H. Jeffery. Middle row: E. Taylor, P. Seaman, P. Parkinson, J. Crane, J. Trow, F. Gillender, P. Lynn, J. Gowland, W. Pattison and W. Clayton. Front row: B. Hewetson, E. Redhead, A. Turnbull, S. Davies, J. Uren, M. Aitken, C. Murray, J. Stokel and M. Westgarth. Staff absent: Mrs Wallace, Mrs Grant and Mrs Bolton.

Jack Uren (1908-97) and Lilian Mary Iley (1911-98)

Jack Uren was born on 8th November 1908 at No 44 William Street, The Lintz. He was christened 'John' but always got 'Jack', even from his pupils. As a boy, he attended the Lintz Methodist Chapel and went to school at what is now Burnopfield Community Centre.

In those days, large families were not unusual and, coming from a family of nine children, he knew poverty and hardship. However, he also knew the importance of family values and these he carried throughout his life. He lived

Jack Uren, 20th July 1934, aged 26.

Lilian Iley, 24th March 1933, aged 22. As a girl, she attended Burnopfield National School, as it was then, directly opposite the chapel. In 1923 she moved to Alderman Wood School in Tanfield, which is now Stanley Comprehensive School (where she would meet Jack).

through the First World War, then in 1926, at the age of 18, he went to a Methodist Teacher Training College in Westminster. He spent two years in London and intended to stay for a third to enable him to complete his degree but he simply couldn't afford it. It was the time of the Depression and he had to start work.

On the 1st January 1936 he married Lilian Iley who he met at Alderman Wood School. Lilian was born at No 1 Gibside Terrace, Busty Bank on 26th July 1911. She was an only child but she would have had a younger brother had he not died at birth.

The main loves of her life, apart from the chapel and her family, were her singing and the Women's Institute. She had a wonderful

Jack and Lilian's wedding day at Burnopfield Methodist Chapel.
On 27th January 1950 Lilian and Jack became the proud parents of John.

soprano voice and, had things worked out differently, she could have sung professionally. As it was, she was in the chapel choir for over 75 years, for which she was very proud to receive a certificate from the Methodist Church Music Society. She was a founder member of Burnopfield Women's Institute, holding every post at some stage. She was its president from November 1975 to November 1978 and one of her highlights was when she attended the Albert Hall at the WI's Golden Jubilee in 1965.

In 1939, when the Second World War broke out, Jack initially joined the Fire Service. In 1941 he joined the Army and immediately told a lie. He was given the choice of joining either the Education Corps or the Signals Corps. Fancying a change from teaching he plumped for the Signals and got in by saying 'yes' when someone asked if he could ride a motor bike. Up to that point he had never even been on one.

He spent the war years as a despatch rider, first travelling throughout the UK and then overseas,

Jack Uren, *circa* 1941.

41

mainly in the Middle East and what was then Palestine. But, even in the Middle East he couldn't escape from Burnopfield. One day after travelling through a desert area he came across a group of British soldiers having something to eat. Riding his motorbike up to them he was amazed to hear a Geordie voice say, 'Wey man, what are ye deing here' – and he found himself face-to-face with Jackie Watson who worked in the Co-op in Burnopfield. During the Second World War, while Jack was serving in the Armed Forces, Lilian did her bit by becoming secretary to the Home Guard until the end of the war. During the war, he reached the rank of sergeant major and he brought a sergeant major's strength of character and determination to his teaching, particularly when he became headmaster of Burnopfield Secondary Modern shortly after their son John was born in 1950. There is no doubt that Jack was strict on standards and discipline at his schools, however, he was always very fair and cared passionately for his students.

Jack had began as a pupil teacher in Flint Hill then left the area briefly to teach first in Birmingham and then in Billingham. However, he was soon back teaching in turn at Beamish, East Stanley, Shield Row and then Burnopfield Secondary Modern School. When Burnopfield became a Junior School in 1967 he took all the pupils to Shield Row where he eventually retired in 1973.

Jack always felt he had to give something back to the community. During his long life he was associated with many local organisations. He held three presidencies, those of Burnopfield Cricket Club, Burnopfield Community Centre and the St John Ambulance Brigade. He was an active member of Stanley Rotary Club – he really enjoyed being part of that organisation – and was a stalwart of Burnopfield Methodist Chapel and its choir – he only had one note but as he said himself, what a note it was. He loved local history and was an expert on Gibside, as a confirmed tee-totaller he delighted in giving talks on pub-signs and of course, he often spoke on Burnopfield. Over the years he assembled the most fascinating and valuable local history archives, a treasure trove of immense importance to the area. Jack's archives were extensively used to produce this book, with the agreement of his son John the archives in their entirety were donated to a very grateful Beamish Museum.

On 28th December 1995 Jack and Lilian received a telegram from the Queen congratulating them on their diamond wedding anniversary.

Jack and Lilian photographed on 1st January 1996 on the occasion of their diamond wedding anniversary.

In August 1997 following a long illness, sadly Jack died – he and Lilian had been married for over 61 years. Lilian had nursed and cared for him until the end, just as she had done when her own mother Maggie tragically died in 1938 and she had to look after her father Jack and his house. Then, when their son John came along in 1950 she had three Johns to look after. Very sadly her father died suddenly, shortly before John's first birthday.

After Jack's death she was lost, she seemed to lose heart, there was no-one left to look after, only herself and she had almost forgotten how to do that.

On 6th August she unveiled a plaque to his memory in Burnopfield Cricket Club and on 13th August, the anniversary of his death, she and her son John attended a beautiful service in St James' Church, Burnopfield, where Jack's ashes were placed in the Garden of Remembrance.

Lilian died quite unexpectedly on 22nd August 1998, her funeral took place on Friday 28th August 1998, close to a year since the death of Jack. Her ashes were placed alongside those of Jack's.

John and Rosemary Uren

John was born on the 27th January 1950 and gained an honours degree and PhD in Civil Engineering. He is currently a senior lecturer at Leeds University and travels the world in the course of his duties.

John met Rosemary Margaret Hill, a Yorkshire girl who was born 26th August 1959 and was formerly a secretary at Leeds University, and they married on the 4th July 1992. They have two wonderful children, John William born 28th April 1995 and Helen Margaret born 23rd February 1997.

John and Rosemary at Whickham in 2001.

Right: John Jnr and Helen in the summer of 2001.

The Baker Family

There has been a Baker family at Burnopfield for at least 150 years. Dealing specifically with the family of recent decades, Polly Baker was formerly Polly Uren and was Jack Uren's full cousin. Jack's father Joseph and Polly's father Jack were brothers. Polly married Leslie Baker (more commonly known as Ted) and they had eight children, six boys and two girls. The Baker Boys were famous in our area long before the Baker Boys of Hollywood fame. Mattie Baker (Ted's cousin) and his wife Doris ran the Grand Cinema admirably for twenty years. One word and a quick flash of the torch from Mattie was enough to silence even the most boisterous of individuals, even courting couples were kept under surveillance to ensure decent behavioural standards.

The Baker family. Left to right: Leslie (2nd August 1932 to 4th August 1996), George (13th December 1937 to 25th June 2000), David (2nd October 1946), Doreen (6th February 1940), Polly – Mother (18th August 1905 to 18th May 1989), Malcolm (15th August 1934), Melvin (15th February 1930) and Colin (14th December 1935). Colin had a twin Ivy who sadly died aged just 2$^{1}/_{2}$ years old. Ted (15th October 1903 to 13th November 1963) died prior to this photograph.

The wedding of Colin Baker to Ethel Jardine of Dunston on 5th September 1959 with Colin's parents Ted and Polly and Ethel's parents Minnie and Jack.

Burnopfield People

It is people who make places and in our previous books we included photographs and stories about ordinary people from the different villages. Our forefathers came to the Durham coalfields seeking work with little or no possessions, most of them were illiterate, their goal was simply to survive and try to create a better future for their children and grandchildren. They endured decades of poverty and oppression, trying desperately to feed and cloth their family against a background of living in slums and working in abominable conditions. People like the coal owners were made fabulously wealthy, thanks to what amounted to little more than slave labour in places like the coal mines. I hope that our forefathers would have been proud of the achievements of so many of their offspring, that better life they sought was created by the constant efforts of successive generations. The next pages demonstrate the efforts many people have made over the years to organise and enrich the community.

Right: The Burnopfield Boys' Brigade on the march.

Burnopfield Scout Troop – first formed around 1931.

Burnopfield Concert Party, *circa* 1930. Jack Uren is fifth from the left, Billy Nelson sixth from left and Tom Mawson first on left.

Burnopfield Women's Fellowship Pageant.

Hobson Chapel Pantomime, *circa* 1920s.

Harlequins Concert Party, 1932. Jack Uren is third from left, back row and Lilian Iley is fourth from left, back row.

I couldn't resist including the following photographs even though very little information exists on some.

Durham Bill, a wonderful photograph, *circa* 1900, of what must be a forerunner in leek show competitions. It is tempting to speculate on who Bill actually was or where the leek show took place, but let the picture speak for itself. The old saying 'it's not the winning that  matters, it's the taking part' is surely true in this case when one looks at the prize trophy. It's almost certain that a collection took place to buy the cup and in those desperately hard up days that's all they could afford.

A group of Burnopfield ladies relaxing in Gibside Woods, *circa* 1900. How nice it would be to know more about them.

The Barrasford triplets. Born 10th October 1901, unfortunately one died and the name is lost. The two survivors were Thomas and Israel. There were also two other sets of twins born into the family, the first set died. Other names we are aware of are Bobby and Matthew who ran a dance band and played at Byermoor Hall. Also in the family were Jane, Frances, Dolly, Lizzy and Kitty. It

is said that there were 22 children in the family. The surviving triplets both worked at the Hobson Colliery and lived in the colliery houses when they married. They eventually moved into bungalows at Garesfield Gardens, The Lintz. Thomas died there but Israel moved to the aged miners' bungalows at Burnopfield, he died 5th October 1976. Israel and his wife Priscilla (née Howe) had children Bob, Dick, Betty, Lydia and Ethel who married Tom Oliphant. It is thanks to Ethel that we have managed to gain information on the triplets.

Judith Forster of Birch Crescent, Burnopfield, pictured here with David Bellamy. Judith's dog used to bring hedgehogs in regularly. The story was featured on the television programme *Bellamy's World*.

Tanfield Parish

The name of Tanfield is derived from the small River Team which flows near it, and 'Feld', Norwegian for fell. Tanfield is therefore the Teamfeld. In some old records Tanfield Lea is spelt Taumfeld Legh. It was also spelt Tamfeld Legh. Tanfield Moor was enclosed and divided in the early part of the last century.

Tanfield, 1910.

This parish formerly embraced the townships of Beamish and Lintz Green, with the villages and hamlets of Tanfield, Shield Row, Stanley, Tantobie, Whit-le-Head, Burnopfield, Lintzford, and Hill Top. A considerable portion of this extensive parish has been used in the formation of new parishes, the last being the parish of Beamish, which takes a large portion from the south-eastern side of the old parish.

The land was chiefly held by Thomas Duncombe Eden, Esq, who was lord of the manor, the executors of the late Sir Henry A. Clavering, the Marquis of Bute, James Joicey Esq JP, Messrs James Joicey & Co, Sir Thomas Thornhill, Miss Ann Jane Allgood, the Earl of Strathmore and the Laycock trustees.

Tanfield in the 1950s.

Tanfield Manor, like Beamish, was at an early period in the possession of Bertram Monboucher, who held it by the payment of one penny, from Robert Conyers. In 1399 the younger Bertram held Tanfield and Cawce (Causey), his heirs continuing to hold the lands till it fell by marriage to Bertram Harbotel, about 1470. Tanfield formed part of the forfeited estates of the unfortunate Earl of Northumberland, in 1569. Within the next thirty years Thomas Harbotel was proprietor of West Tanfield and shortly after, the estate came into the Shafto family, who in turn conveyed it to William Kennet, Esq. In later years the Dawsons are given as proprietors and was then held by Thomas Duncombe Eden, Esq.

Tanfield was known for its coal in an early period of the coal mining industry. In the time of the Commonwealth a portion of Tanfield Moor Colliery was sold by Cromwell, that is, the bishop's rights on the same. The Causey Arch was built in 1727, to carry coals from pits in the neighbourhood of Tanfield to the Staithes on the Tyne. The first coals from the little colliery at Tanfield Moor were conveyed to the staithes at Derwent Haugh and were considered by judges to be equal in quality to any coals brought to the River Tyne.

St Margaret's Church.

The church is a picturesque stone building, dedicated to St Margaret, and occupies a pleasant situation east of the village. It is of very ancient foundation, being one of the early chapelries of Chester-le-Street. The church was almost entirely rebuilt in 1749 and has since been several times restored and improved, so that of the original chapel there remain only portions of the chancel and the north wall. During the restorations of 1877, an ancient piscina was discovered and is now built into the north wall of the chancel. The church consists of nave, aisles, chancel, and massive square embattled tower, the latter being added in 1853, by John Eden. The parish register has been lost or destroyed up to 1719.

Tommy Armstrong – Tanfield's Pitman's Poet

Some time ago a local man, Brian Robson, asked if I would be interested in seeing an old photograph of his great-grandfather accompanied by his old watch. I copied the picture and photographed the old watch, they meant little to me but I filed them for further investigation. I now know that Brian's great-grandfather was Tommy Armstrong the Pitman's Poet and I had been lucky enough to have access to possibly the only original photograph of him and of course his antique watch. I obtained much of the following information from the book *Tommy Armstrong Sings* by Tom Gilfellon.

Tommy was born on 15th August 1848 at Wood Street, Shotley Bridge. In the early 1850s the family moved to South Pontop and then on to East Tanfield. Tommy worked at South Pontop and East Tanfield Collieries. Born fighting, he worked through his poetry and music against poverty and injustice all of his days.

The Pitman's Poet.

He left school at nine years of age and like most young lads went to work at the pit, often having to be carried there by his older brother William because of the pain in his short, bent legs. At the age of twelve he was a pony lad and in all probability was already composing verse, it is probable that during the hours spent underground the lads sang to keep their spirits up. The trapper lads who kept the ventilation doors were most inventive, given to improvising satirical verses about their older workmates.

It was after the move to South Pontop, near Annfield Plain, that he attended his first concert where he heard and was most impressed by a local comedian, Mr MacMillan, and a rising star in the then booming Tyneside music halls, Joe Wilson. He was moved to write a song about Mr MacMillan. This was to be a typical Armstrong song, about local events and characters. His songs were chronicles, for and about the people of his area. He rarely set his sights on the lucrative music hall circuit in Newcastle, not that he was unaware of what his more famed contemporaries in Newcastle were up to. He was never above appropriating one of their compositions, changing names and places to suit his locale and singing it as his own.

The most famous example of this being 'Nanny's a Maisor' which is still a Tyneside standard. Nanny was originally Peggy and her ill-fated trip was to have been to Sunderland.

Song writing was seriously rivalled in the young Armstrong's affections by quoits playing, at which he was a local champion and much of his time was spent at this pastime behind the

Tommy Armstrong's watch.

Shield Row Hotel where there was a quoits pitch and a skittle alley. Song writing must have gained upper hand because as he was never far away waiting to capitalize on the opportunity of composing some new song or poem.

About 1866 Tommy found himself in trouble when he was arrested by police officers at Addison Colliery near Blaydon. He had written some poetry for funeral cards which an old door to door hawker had agreed to have printed and framed for a certain sum. However, upon delivery of the goods he overcharged one of his brothers two shillings which angered Tommy. He was a fiery man and seeking retribution he waylaid the hawker the next time he came round, trapped him in the house and threatened to kill him. The old man was terrified and when he was set free immediately went to the police and demanded Tommy's arrest. Freedom for Tommy came only after spending three days in Blaydon police station and he never recovered his money!

By 1870 Tommy was famous throughout the Stanley area not only as a poet but as an entertainer too and had formed his own concert party. Tommy himself was no singer, nor did he ever profess to be, in fact his musical ability was, to say the least, limited. His greatest asset as a performer was his razor sharp wit which, with his gift for improvisation of verse, ensured that he was never at a loss for words. With his disguises and his short, bandy legs he could reduce an audience to helpless laughter by the simple process of standing silently on stage for a minute or two.

He had a family of fourteen and a considerable appetite for beer, Tommy had his poems printed and sold them at a penny a time in order to pay for his drink and in its turn the beer often inspired new creations.

With the fame of his concert party growing Tommy was a busy man but it was well known that he would always find the time to bring his talents to the aid of any charitable cause in the locality. His troupe performed at and organised innumerable functions to raise money for victims of misfortune and pit disaster, for reading rooms and the funds of the struggling miners' union. His work was committed to improving the lot of the miner and displayed a profound class consciousness, a noticeable faculty for criticism of society. The 1880s and '90s was a militant period when the membership of the miners' federation rose dramatically to 200,000. Strikes and lockouts were frequent and the pitmen were at last combining to present a solid front to the coal owners. Their movement was by no means revolutionary, nor did it have any long-term ideological goals and the pitmen's attitude is mirrored in their songs of the period, wherein they call for the redress of immediate grievances. These songs also served a practical purpose in as much as they also raised money for the hungry families of strikers when they were sung in the streets. They illustrated the harsh conditions of the miner's employ and showed a hearty disgust for the greed of the employers and emphasised the striker's resolution

Tommy's gravestone.

to see the job through. Tommy often pilloried individuals whom he thought merited such treatment. The song 'Oakey's Keeker' was written about one Joe Elliott a new overseer or 'keeker' at Maiden Law drift pit. Elliott took out a private prosecution before the Lanchester magistrates seeking redress for the libel. He presented them with a print of the poem as evidence, but to his increased annoyance, the Clerk of the Court and the magistrates had smiles of amusement on their faces. Enquiring closer of Elliott as to what in particular he objected to in the poem, the magistrates were told that 'He called me a 'hairy faced rascal'. 'Well,' said the Clerk of the Court, 'You still have your whiskers'. The following day the last two verses of the poem as it is today, appeared.

Never a rich man, Tommy suffered more and more from want in his declining years. Concert parties and entertainments were arranged to assist him, little enough for a man who had kept Stanley laughing for fifty years. He died at Tantobie on 30th August 1920 at the age of seventy-two. A few lines from his poem 'The Durham Lockout' are engraved on his tombstone:

*The miners of Northumberland
we shall for ever praise,
For being so kind in helping us
those tyrannising days;
We thank the other counties too,
that have been doing the same
For every man who reads will
know that we are not to blame.*

The tombstone was unveiled on 9th August 1986 by Arthur Scargill, President of the National Union of Mineworkers.

The Trimdon Grange Explosion

Let us not think of tomorrow,
Lest we disappointed be;
All our joys may turn to sorrow,
As we all may daily see.
Today we may be strong and healthy,
But how soon there comes a change,
As we may learn from the explosion,
That has been at Trimdon Grange.

Men and boys left home that morning,
For to earn their daily bread,
Little thought before that evening
That they'd be numbered with the dead;
Let us think of Mrs Burnett,
Once had sons but now has none,
By the Trimdon Grange explosion,
Joseph, George and James are gone.

February left behind it
What will never be forgot;
Weeping widows, helpless children,
May be found in many a cot,
Homes that once were blest with comfort.
Guided by a father's care,
Now are solemn, sad and gloomy,
Since the father is not there.

Little children, kind and loving,
From their homes each day would run
For to meet their father's coming,
As each hard day's work was done.
Now they ask if father's left them,
Then the mother hangs her head;
With a weeping widow's feelings,
Tells the child that 'father's dead.'

God protect the lonely widow,
Help to raise each drooping head;
Be a Father to the orphans,
Never let them cry for bread.
Death will pay us all a visit,
They have only gone before;
We may meet the Trimdon victims
Where explosions are no more.

Written to commemorate the 74 men and boys who lost their lives in 1882.

GIBSIDE

The Column of British Liberty at Gibside.

Gibside was the Jacobean house of William Blakiston (rebuilt around 1805). George Bowes formed around 1730-60 the once famous landscape park of which buildings in part remain. After 1890 the house was occupied only intermittently. In 1936-39 the woods were felled, the house having been dismantled in 1920.

Right: An engraving after a painting by Turner, taken from the top of the park shows the landscape as it was 150 years ago, with the long low Tudor house below in the middle distance, the Column of Liberty on its hill to the right, and the mausoleum on the extreme left. All accounts, from the middle of the eighteenth century to that of the nineteenth, suggest that Turner scarcely exaggerated the picturesque magnificence of the domain.

The first recorded owners of this stretch of forest on the border of Durham and Northumberland were the Marley family, who held it in 1230. They so continued till 1540, when the estate passed by marriage to Roger Blakiston of Coxhoe. Gibside remained the home of his descendants till 1713, when Sir Francis Blakiston, was succeeded by his only daughter, Elizabeth, who had married Sir William Bowes of Streatlam Castle, between Barnard Castle and Raby. The Bowes family, by tradition taking their name, and their arms of three long bows, from one William who, in 1089 was given charge of Bowes Castle, had possessed Streatlam since 1300. After the union of the two estates Streatlam was rebuilt in a striking Baroque manner and Gibside was deserted until Sir William's younger son, George, came into both estates in 1721.

George Bowes, the county's MP from 1734 till his death, must also have been an artist sensitive to the romance of Gibside, since he devoted so much of his life to perfecting its landscapes. The house itself, backing on to the steep

descent to the valley, was essentially that built by William Blakiston under James I, possibly incorporating yet earlier parts. The south front (*left*) is stated to have been rebuilt around 1805 by Bowes' grandson, John Lyon, 10th Earl of Strathmore. Certainly the exaggeratedly high battlemented parapet, was added at that date.

The porch (*right*), bears the initials of William and Jane Blakiston, with the date 1625 and his arms quartering Marley. Above are the Royal Arms of James I, flanked by admirably sculptured figures that may well be by the same carver, probably Flemish, as those at Chillingham Castle in Northumberland, and have been retained in situ.

It was thought that the restoration of the house in 1805 and other work about the place of that epoch may be the earliest work of John Dobson (1787-1865), the famous Newcastle architect. But David Stephenson, then leading builder and architect on the Tyne and his master, is more likely to have handled the work if a local man was employed.

From the east end of the house a glade through the woods was aligned on the Column of British Liberty which also terminates the east end of a grass terrace or avenue, a mile long, at the western end of which was placed the mausoleum (*below*).

Between house and column, but concealed from the former by a belt of trees, is the stable court (*right*). From the same point, looking south, there is the view of the Gothic banqueting house (*below*) overlooking a multi-angular pool.

Parallel with and below the terrace avenue ran the western approach to the house, through an extensive lawn, and past the walled kitchen garden. On the north side of these stands the orangery (*opposite page facing*), a bow in the north side of which overlooks the valley.

There is no evidence that any professional gardener was employed at Gibside, but Bowes may have gained inspiration from the gardens of Castle Howard. But the genius that adapted their pattern of divergent avenues centred on monumental buildings, to this heavily wooded and violently contoured site was almost certainly his alone.

The Column, 140 ft high, was begun in 1750 and completed in 1757 at the cost of £2,000, built entirely by estate labour except for the surmounting figure. The sculptor in 1756 of the 12 ft high statue was Christopher Richardson, who carved the figure on the spot.

The magnificent domed chapel (*right*) and mausoleum, at the west end of the terrace-avenue was not begun till 1760, when Bowes was already aware of his approaching death. A clause to his will, appointed his trustees to expend £1,000 in completing it within six years, of his death, but it was not finished

and consecrated till 1812 by his grandson. By then Gibside and Streatlam had become parts of the widespread estates of the Earls of Strathmore, though from 1820 to 1860 Gibside was settled on the dowager of the 10th Earl and her second husband, by whom the place was fully maintained. In 1885, following the death of John Bowes, Gibside reverted to the Earls of Strathmore, the Bowes-Lyon family. After that date the house was only intermittently occupied, and probably never by any of the Earls. During the First World War Land Army girls were billeted in the house, which, lacking plumbing or sanitation, and the roof becoming unsafe, was dismantled in 1920. In 1930-39 the woods were felled and in 1954 the Forestry Commission leases were signed. In 1966 the National Trust restored the chapel and the Queen Mother attended a special service.

Mary Eleanor Countess of Strathmore

One of the most interesting chapters in the history of Gibside concerned Eleanor – the only child of George Bowes of Streathlam – and one Andrew Robinson Stoney. The name is not so familiar now, but the subject was much more familiar to earlier residents of the district. At that time the name of Bowes could not be mentioned without reference to, or the name connected with, Stoney Bowes.

In the first place, he was neither a Bowes nor a Strathmore. He came to Newcastle around 1770, as an ensign in the 4th Regiment of Foot. His first wife was the daughter of William Newton of Burnopfield. The Newtons had made a great deal of money in the coal trade, and lived at first in a house at Dyke Heads. He built the house at Burnopfield which belonged to the late Dr Watson. Stoney is said to have persuaded Miss Newton to elope with him from this house. Miss Newton's fortune was £30,000. They were married at St Andrew's Church, Newcastle, by the Rev Nathaniel Ellison. This lady died leaving no issue, having, according to common report, endured much suffering at the hands of her husband. After her death, Lieutenant Stoney began to have designs on the hand of Eleanor, the young widow of John Lyon 9th Earl of Strathmore.

This lady was a very talented person, an accomplished botanist, a good linguist, and a poet. While her father, George Bowes, lived, she had spent many a happy and pleasant day among the shady woods of Gibside, and would look back upon them with regret and fondness. After the death of the Earl she lived at Chelsea, where she had extensive conservatories and vineries. Here she was paid attention to by a gentleman just returned from India, of similar tastes to her own, and might probably have married him, had not the young adventurer

Andrew Robinson Stoney, come on to the scene. The *Morning Post* was then the fashionable society paper. In this paper several articles appeared from time to time insinuating that the young widow was not leading her life so innocently as to meet with the approval of the more rigorous moralists of the times. The correspondence led to a duel being fought between the editor of the paper and Lieutenant Stoney as the champion of the Countess. The gallantry of the Lieutenant was rewarded by the Countess marrying him four days later. It transpired, however, that Stoney himself had sent the articles reflecting on the Countess, and had also written those defending her. The duel was a sham, and that an understanding existed all the time between the editor and Stoney which throws quite a different light on the affair. No matter, the end was secured and Stoney had become the husband of the Countess of Strathmore.

A portrait of Mary Eleanor Bowes.
Born 24th February 1749.

The expensive living of Andrew (Stoney) Bowes soon forced him to leave Gibside. He had all but bankrupted Eleanor except for her shrewd investments prior to her marriage. He had even cut down much valuable timber to raise money, but no one would buy from him. He began to treat the Countess as he had treated his former wife. He used to lock her up in a closet and feed her only an egg and a biscuit a day.

In order to obtain more influence over the Countess, Bowes took away one of her daughters by Lord Strathmore to Paris. This was the Lady Anna Maria, afterwards the wife of Colonel Jessop. But the young lady, being a ward in Chancery, was brought back by the Court. The following year, 1785, the Countess fled from his custody, and began to institute proceedings for a divorce.

It appeared from the evidence in the case, that shortly after her marriage she had been deprived of her liberty in every respect. The use of her carriage was denied to her unless with Stoney Bowes' special permission. Her own

Andrew Robinson Stoney. His name coined the expression 'Stoney Broke'.

servants were dismissed and new ones engaged. She could not write a letter nor receive one without his knowledge or his knowing the contents. She was driven from her own table, or forced to sit at it along with Bowes' mistresses. While the divorce suit was pending, Bowes carried her off to Streatlam Castle and endeavoured to persuade her to be reconciled to him. Being pursued from London, Bowes hastily made off from Streatlam, carrying her with him. He was overtaken at Darlington, and the Countess was freed. Proceedings were immediately instituted against him and he was bound over to keep the peace in sureties of himself for £10,000 and two sureties of £5,000 each.

Bowes' trial took place on Wednesday, 10th May 1787. The trial was for a conspiracy against Lady Strathmore to assault and imprison her. Various evidence of ill-usage were given, and the result was that Bowes had to pay a fine of £300, to be imprisoned for three years and to keep the peace for fourteen years. At the same time a trial against him took place, brought on by Lady Strathmore, to set aside the deed by transferred rents and other property to Bowes. This was successful, and he was deprived of all the property, and the whole of the rents which he had received. He was cast into prison, where he died on the 16th June 1810.

The Countess of Strathmore was restored to her property and severed from the unfortunate connection she had formed. She died in April 1800 and was buried in Westminster Abbey, dressed in a superb bridal dress. Her tombstone may be seen in Poet's Corner, the inscription reads: 'Sacred to the memory of Mary Eleanor, Countess of Strathmore, of Streatlam and Gibside, in the County of Durham.'

John Bowes 1811-1885

The Earl of Strathmore, who married Miss Mary Eleanor Bowes, only daughter of George Bowes, left issue two sons and three daughters, the eldest son of course succeeding to the title and estates. This was John, 10th Earl of Strathmore and Kinghorn, who was born in 1769. This John married on Sunday, 30th July 1820, Miss Mary Milner of Staindrop, mother of the late John Bowes Esq. After his lordship's death, this lady married, on the 16th March 1831, William Hutt Esq who became MP for Gateshead and was afterwards knighted. Sir William and Lady Strathmore lived at Gibside and occasionally in London, until Lady Strathmore's death in May 1860. She died in London and her remains were brought to Gibside and placed in the family mausoleum underneath the chapel. Sir William subsequently married again and shortly afterwards left Gibside.

Mr John Bowes, son of Lord Strathmore, succeeded to the English estates on coming of age, but the Scottish estates went to the Strathmore family. Mr Bowes lived mostly in Paris. He was Member of Parliament for fifteen years for the Southern Division of the County of Durham. He married his first wife, Josephine Benoite, Countess of Montalbo, in about 1852. Before her death, Mr Bowes commenced to build the magnificent mansion at Barnard Castle, intended to have been, in event of Mr Bowes predeceasing the Countess, a residence for her, and afterwards to be presented to the town of Barnard Castle as a museum of art and curiosities. But the Countess died on 18th August 1874, and her remains were brought to Gibside and placed underneath the chapel.

John, 10th Earl of Strathmore (1769-1820). Son of Mary Eleanor.

Mary Milner – died May 1860.

John Bowes, 1811-85.

Josephine Benoite Countess of Montalbo.

Three years after the death of his wife, on the 18th August 1877, John Bowes married another French lady, Alphonsine Comptesse de Courten, although their marriage soon ended in separation. He died in October, 1885, when his remains were placed in the family vault underneath the chapel. In 1928 the remains of John and Josephine Benoite were removed from Gibside and taken to Barnard Castle. Upon the death of John Bowes in 1885, Gibside reverted to the Earls of Strathmore, the Bowes-Lyon family, specifically into the possession of his cousin. And so to the linear descendents of Thomas Lyon Bowes, the 11th Earl of Strathmore.

Alphonsine, John Bowes' second wife.

Streatlam and the Bowes

The original structure of Streatlam Castle near Barnard Castle was erected by the Baliolis and was for many generations the residence of the owners of the manor. It was rebuilt from the ground in 1450 by Sir William Bowes and sustained a siege of seven days during the Northern Rebellion. On its eventual capture by the rebels the castle was completely gutted, everything that could be moved was taken away. The castle was rebuilt on the site of the old one in the beginning of the 1700s. It was an elegant stone building with a southern aspect.

On 25th June 1841 the Victorian writer William Makepeace Thackeray and a friend of John Bowes, described the interior of the castle. It had 24 bedrooms, three drawing rooms, a lounge dining room, libraries and a billiard room. Portraits of the Bowes family hung in the corridors. Thackeray also tells of the fine colts and mares of the successful racing stock owned by

George Bowes (1701-60) of Streatlam and Gibside, MP for Durham.

John Bowes. The castle was demolished in 1927 following a piecemeal sale. The final ruins of the castle were blasted to smithereens by the Territorial Army in 1959 as part of a technical exercise.

Streatlam Castle – now demolished.

The Bowes Museum

Life-size portraits of John Bowes and Josephine Countess of Montalbo face visitors in the entrance hall, and within the museum their lives and activities are illustrated by photographs and by a number of their personal possessions.

The Bowes collections were formed from the 1840s to the 1870s. The present museum built specially to house them, not as a private residence, though a suite of rooms on the upper floors was reserved for the Countess of Montalbo, the title acquired by Mrs Bowes.

Adjoining the market town of Barnard Castle, the site was the nearest convenient one to John Bowes' ancestral home three miles away at Streatlam Castle (now demolished). The massive building was designed in 1869, mainly by a French architect. It has been called perhaps the best example in Britain of the Second Empire style. The museum

The entrance hall.

was opened in 1892, sadly by then the founders were deceased. In 1956 the trustees handed over the museum and its collections to the Durham County Council in the presence of Queen Elizabeth the Queen Mother.

The impressive Bowes Museum.

A Wedding at Gibside

On Sunday 22nd May 1988 there was a historic first wedding at Gibside Chapel. Bride Joanne Clarke was carried by horse drawn carriage to and from the chapel with its strong family connections with the Queen Mother.

Joanne and her New Zealander husband Patrick Roxburgh needed special permission to marry in the mausoleum where the Queen Mother's ancestors are buried. And in another history making event it was the first time a horse drawn carriage was allowed on the training race course leading to the chapel.

Joanne, aged 22, was the daughter of the chapel's custodian Joan Gardener. She had always wanted to be married there since her mother took the job.

Joanne, who was an assistant in a London perfume shop, said she was delighted to marry in the chapel. The ceremony was conducted by chaplain Canon Tony Meakin who said the couple had permission from the Archbishop of Canterbury because the church was not normally licensed for weddings. He also needed the permission of the Earl of Strathmore, the Queen Mother's nephew, because of the family connections.

Joanne's mother had fell in love with the chapel many years ago and was thrilled that they were able to use it for Joanne's wedding. Joanne's bridesmaids also arrived in a horse drawn open carriage. The reception was held in a marquee in the chapel grounds.

SECTION THREE

BYERMOOR AND FELLSIDE

Byermoor Brownies: Lesley Dillon, Anne Malone, Sheila Gill, Ann Baker, unknown, Mary Allison, Joan Hagan and Cecilia Smith.

Byermoor Coal Mining
A Glimpse of the Early Days

Byermoor, one mile west of Marley Hill, is a village where coal mining has been carried on for hundreds of years. The village is very old, being mentioned, in the Boldon Book (1183), as Beechermoor. At the time Phillip de Gildford owned Byermoor, his family also possessed the Manor of Collierley (now Dipton) and held it until the failure of male issue in 1474, when their estates passed by marriage to the Robsons.

The mines at Byermoor were owned and worked by Sir Thomas Clavering in 1740. Records of the working of these old pits still exist. The Byermoor Pit pay bill for the fortnight ending 20th February 1770 gives some interesting details of the wages paid. The colliery employed 18 hands, 10 hewers and 8 putters. The hewers being paid at the rate of 1 shilling per score of corves, while the putters got 9 pence per score. The total quantity of coal raised for the fortnight of nine days was 162 score and five corves, for which the hewers received £8 2s 3d and the putters £6 1s 8¹/₄d. When it is explained that a corf contained 12 pecks or 54 gallons of coal, it will enable those interested in wages, to note the difference between the wages paid in modern days prior to pit closures and those paid to Byermoor pitmen in 1770.

A bond dated 1779 tells us how the pits were worked. It is an agreement between Sir Thomas Clavering and the hewers and putters of Andrews House and Byermoor Pits. The hewers received 22 shillings binding money, and half a guinea was paid to the putters. The coals wrought by the men were filled into a corf or wicker basket on a sledge from the workings to the shaft. As the workings extended, putting became expensive. This led to the introduction of wooden rails and the invention of a sort of tram on wheels. This was the system in vogue at Byermoor in 1779. The wooden tub was not introduced until the year 1797, by John Curr of Sheffield. John Curr was originally a local man, born near West Kyo, the son of John Curr, head viewer at Bushblades Pit. The terms of the agreement at Andrews House and Byermoor were as follows. The hewers at the first named pit were to receive 1s 9d per score for the whole coal, two shillings for the whole coal under the top, 1s 8d and 1s 6d for the pillars and eight pence a yard for headways in the whole mine and sixpence a yard for the pillars.

For every score wrought at Byermoor, one shilling was paid and four pence a yard for headways. The drivers were to put the coal and assist the hewers in filling at a fixed rate of one shilling per day. The men promised not to neglect their work and agree to forfeit one shilling for every day lost through neglect.

Byermoor Pit, *circa* 1900.

They were also under a penalty to keep their coals clean from stones. A viewer had the supervision of a number of pits at this time, and as very small salary was paid, his visits would be very few. The sum paid to John Ramsay for viewing Byermoor for two years was seven guineas.

In 1710 Thomas Browell of Newcastle, obtained a lease from Sir John Clavering to build a waggonway from Byermoor to the Tyne, he

A Byermoor miner pushing a tub to the cage in the late 1800s.

intended to use iron rails. This is of special interest, because it was sixty years before the first iron railway was laid at Coalbrookdale, near Ironbridge, Shrewsbury. Expensive lawsuits prevented this bold pioneer from carrying out his intentions. But for these lawsuits, Byermoor would have been the first place where an iron railway was laid in the country. This would have been of great historical importance in a district where the first railway was laid by the Liddels of Ravensworth in 1671 and in which the famous Causey Arch, the oldest surviving railway viaduct was built in 1726.

A miner, again in the late 1800s, pictured beside the cage weight. In later years the weight was replaced with a further cage as a counter balance.

Byermoor School

We were fortunate indeed to be given a collection of photographs by Mrs Gertrude Alice Kelly (née Kehoe and always known as Alice) daughter of Thomas Kehoe (granddaughter of Michael Kehoe, Chairman of Whickham Council) and the niece of James and Alice Kehoe who were Byermoor teachers. We are able to include but a sample of the collection.

Many teachers have passed through Byermoor School, all with individual qualities and all remembered by pupils for a variety of reasons. Miss Clare Arnold is perhaps one of the best known teachers and certainly the oldest surviving one. Held in great affection by all who know her, she celebrated her 91st birthday in May 2002.

Clare Arnold, *circa* 1920. Still respectfully referred to as Miss Arnold, she was born in Burnopfield on 13th May 1911. She attended Byermoor School, Darlington Convent School and Liverpool College. Miss Arnold taught at schools in the Lake District, Tanfield Lea and Byermoor Sacred Heart School. She retired in 1976 after a long career.

Byermoor School class, 1913. Including: Aileen Arnold, Josephine McCreish, Ann Bradley, Lena Clark, Anastasia Clark, Elizabeth Clark, Sadie Clark and Ella Duffy. It is difficult to identify pupils from over 50 years ago but thanks to Sheila McGahon's efforts we are able to name some. No doubt members of the community will spot friends and relatives. Our sincere apologies to those we are unable to identify.

Children at a school concert in 1949. Girls: Margaret Joyce, Jean Cairns, Mary Connor, Mary Boland, Sheila Graham, Ann Greener, Ann Dunphy, Barbara Cairns, Mary Hanratty and Winnie Cairns. Boys: Michael McKenna, Tom Callaghan, Timothy Doran, Vincent McTaff, Frank Campbell, David Young, Tom Smith, Kelvin McHugh, John Gavin and Edward Bond.

Class 2, August 1949. Back row: Kevin Jobson, Frank Campbell, Kathleen Gowan, Jean Cairns, Ann McGinn, Mary Grimes, Kathleen Joyce, unknown, unknown, Winifred Cairns, Matthew Collins and John Harbron. Middle row: Ann Greener, Mary Mountford, Rose McCormick, Margaret Joyce, Mary Boland, unknown, Ann McTaff and Mary Boland. Front row: unknown, Harvey Boland, unknown, unknown, Michael McKenna, Gerard Boland, unknown, Wilf Prinn and Tom Callaghan.

Class 4, August 1949. Included are: Lilian Brown, Tom Carrick, Derek Armstrong, Tom Hall, Joseph O'Rourke, Tom Hanratty, Austin Dunphy, ? Lynch, Aileen O'Rourke, Teresa Boyd, Ann Boyd, Stephanie Boland and Cecily Clark.

Class 5, August 1949. Pupils include: Billy McGarry, Margaret Callaghan, Gerard Joyce, Joanna Campbell, Genevieve Young, Brian Phelps, Raymond Phelps, Deirdre Hepple and Kathleen Carrick.

The teaching staff of Byermoor School have been well photographed over the years, it never ceases to amaze us though, how every now and then a new photograph is unearthed. The teachers pictured are, standing left to right: Mr White, Miss Clark, Miss Kehoe and Mr Henry. Seated are: Miss Mulcahy and Miss Arnold.

A class from around 1952, pictured on the field at the side of the school with teacher Mr Smith. Some of the pupils present are, boys: Tom McGee, Alan Longstaff, Billy Hall, Hughie McGinn, Tom Carrick, Paul O'Rourke, Derek Bond, Alan Nash and Tony Doran. Girls: Anne Joyce, Sheila McTaff, Kathleen Brabban, Monica Hagan, Aileen O'Rourke and Catharine McGee.

Over the years Byermoor teacher Mrs Alice Kehoe collected and treasured class photographs. Thanks to her niece Mrs Alice Kelly (née Kehoe) those photographs have been passed on to our history society. Two particularly good photographs are of Class 1 boys and girls taken in August 1949.

Back row: Monica Grimes, Pat Wake, Kathleen Ratcliffe, Lucy Bradley, Eileen Dunphy and Sheila McMahon. Front row: Mary Callaghan, Pauline Lyons, Mary Brabban, Patricia Heslin, Clare McTaff and Ann Young.

Back row: Terence O'Rourke, Norman James, Stephen Grant, John Bradley, James Boland, Aidan Brough, John Donnelly and Gordon Tully. Front row: Edmund Smith, Leo Bradley, John Boland and Matthew Collins.

The Kehoe Family

The present school at Byermoor dates from 1883. The average attendance was 130 pupils in 1890 and 165 pupils in 1906. In January 1913 gas lighting was installed in the school.

Mr James Kehoe (1906-58) was headmaster at the school and his sister Alice was also a teacher here. Their sister Gertrude was a teacher at St Joseph's School, Blaydon. They all lived at 'Fairfield', The Crescent.

Their father was Michael Kehoe (1861-1920) of Church Street, a colliery mason. He was secretary of Marley Hill branch of the Durham Colliery Mechanics Association for twenty years and served on Whickham Council and on the Blaydon District Education Sub Committee. In the 1920s the Kehoe sisters had a milliners shop at No 17 Granby Terrace, Sunniside.

Alice Kelly (née Kehoe), the niece of headmaster James Kehoe, very kindly donated photographs of the Kehoe family and Byermoor School classes.

Members of the Kehoe family. Standing: Maggie Graham, John Robert Kehoe and Alice Kehoe. Seated: Winnie Clark, Alice Kehoe (grandmother) and Mary Kehoe.

Councillor Michael Kehoe, third from left seated on the lower level of the carriage, outside Whickham UDC offices.

Byermoor the Community

The following pictures are from slides taken by Father Wright who was curate at Byermoor Sacred Heart Church in the 1960s. When he died his collection of slides was eventually handed to Sheila McGahon. It is unfortunate that we are unable to feature more in this book. The slides have been put to good use however, with the help of Sunniside & District Local History Society they have been displayed on social evenings to help fund raise for the church and school.

The Catholic Women's League. Back row: Mrs Batey, Mary Herron and Lilian Doran. Front row: Miss Kilkenny, Mary O'Rourke and Aileen Arnold.

On 23rd April 1947 Mary Donnelly married Thomas Gerard (Gerry) Herron who was a tradesman working for the NCB. He was also a Whickham Urban District Labour Councillor, and an avid trade unionist. Gerry was a great orator, never using notes but speaking from the heart. As a councillor he was a true servant of the people, always willing to listen and discuss problems, even when on a social evening out at the local club. Many had cause to be very grateful to him for his efforts and staunch support. In the 1970s he almost defeated Giles Radice when he sought selection as the Labour Party candidate to fight the seat of MP for Chester-le-Street. At a time when the Labour Party dominated the area, in the view of the author, he was the community's greatest socialist councillor and trade union leader. Gerry died on 9th July 2000. At his funeral in Byermoor Sacred Heart Church, probably for the first time, that great Socialist anthem *The Red Flag* was sung with great gusto.

Mr Henry (Harry) Gardner, former headmaster of Byermoor School with Mrs Gardner, Elaine Gardner and school meals staff: Sheila McGahon, Mrs Proctor and Mrs Boland, May 1967.

Children at Byermoor. West Farm (now demolished) is to the left rear and the council houses to the right.

Lads at play with the now demolished Byermoor Colliery houses in the background. Unfortunately we are unable to identify any of the lads.

A May procession leaving Byermoor Sacred Heart Church in the 1960s.

Youth Hut

During the 1940s, Father Pickering purchased a large wooden hut, which had formerly belonged to the local Boys' Club at Marley Hill. It was transported in sections from Marley Hill to Byermoor and erected near the Parish Hall. The building, after completion was then used primarily by youth organisations for the benefit of young people within the community, enabling

The youth hut with the Church Hall to the left. Both have been demolished.

them to take part in the various sporting activities such as boxing, judo and gymnastics. They proved to be very popular with youngsters and many an enjoyable night was spent at the hut, with boys and girls taking advantage of the facilities open to them.

Along with these activities the hut was also used as a venue for the local boys and girls clubs, the girl guides and boy scouts associations.

The amenities consisted of one large room, two small rooms and a shower room. Late in the 1960s the hut was used temporarily as an extra classroom for the school. After many years of useful service to the community, the building began to deteriorate and by the 1970s, it was finally demolished.

The history of Byermoor Church has been well documented and arguably the most popular priest was Father Austin Pickering who died 24th April 1968 at the great age of 87 years. Almost as well known by local people, were other famous residents of Byermoor Church grounds, Father Pickering's peacocks. He is shown here encouraging one to feed from his hand.

The altar of Byermoor Sacred Heart Church as well as being the ultimate religious symbol, is nothing short of a beautiful work of art. It is shown here in all its glory during the Consecration of the Church by Bishop McCormack on 9th October 1948, Father Austin Pickering was parish priest.

Church processions were very much a part of life, as well as the religious significance of the event, it was an opportunity for parents to dress their children up in all their finery. This photograph taken in the early 1930s even though a time of great poverty, shows

how conscientiously parents applied themselves in ensuring that no expense was spared when dressing their children appropriately for the occasion. Some of those pictured are: Patty Murray, M. Henry, T. Hearne, A. Kehoe, Mary Bell, D. Walker and Joan Kennedy.

Fellside

In the nineteenth century Fellside consisted of around fourteen houses and a couple of farms, standing on the edge of Whickham Fell, just within the Earl of Strathmore's estate. Fellside gave its name to one of the quarters of Whickham parish in connection with civil administration affairs, such as they were in the eighteenth and nineteenth centuries. The Fellside quarter was basically all the high ground to the south west of Whickham – ie Hollinside and Riding Barns, Gibside and Marley Hill, Byermoor and Crookgate, Old Sunniside and Whickham Fell. Over at Lamesley Chapelry, the divisions were known as townships, while at Tanfield they were known as constabularies. The road, so far as locals were concerned, began at Crookgate and ended at Whickham.

Fellside Chapel and Houses

Shortly before he died, Mr Thomas Hewitt, a Newcastle draper and a resident of Hunters Hill, built a Wesleyan Chapel close by in 1875. Tom's wife Isabella, continued to live at Hunters Hill until 1882.

To get one's bearings and using the Woodmans Arms as a reference point, Hunters Hill was on the opposite side of the road. The chapel was directly opposite the Woodmans Arms, also on the other side of the road.

Fellside Chapel.

The small Wesleyan Chapel was built of brick at a cost of £250 and could, at a squeeze, seat 150 people. A porch and vestry were attached. Behind the pulpit, high up on the gable wall, was a circular window depicting the Lamb of God. An American organ with foot pedals was obtained by the members and in the 1920s was played by Stanton Bone. Oil lamps lit the chapel in winter. Services were held up until 1970 when the chapel was demolished.

Demolition of the chapel in 1970.

On the south side of Fellside Road in 1858 were four cottages, some gardens and a saw pit. Two cottages remained standing but derelict up to 1965. Tom Ismay (1890-1974), lived there until his retirement in 1955. He worked at the Whinfield Coke Ovens, Rowlands Gill, and walked to work via Gibside Wood with the consent of the Bailiff. On the north side was the chapel and a short row of four stone houses.

The houses with the chapel to the left. The houses had mains water but no gas or electricity, there were earth closets (middens) at the end of the row. They were vacated in 1937 as unfit to live in. Jack Guthrie lived in one of the houses in the early 1930s and he walked to work over the fields to Marley Hill Pit, where he was in charge of the pumps.

Bird Hill House, Fellside

Bird Hill Close is mentioned in a will of 1603 and may have got its name from a nearby rookery. A map drawn about 1722, now in Durham Record Office, marks Bird Hill and the waggonways at Fawdon Fields. George Bowes owned the area in 1745 and in 1807 the Earl of Strathmore paid one shilling and eight pence church rate for Bird Hill House. Lady Anna Maria Jessup, daughter of the Earl of Strathmore, lived here from 1810, until her death in 1832. In 1787, at the age of 17, she eloped with a young lawyer, Henry Jessup (styled as Colonel Jessup in 1825) and was married at Gretna Green. Their daughter Susan married John Davidson of Ridley Hall, Bardon Mill, whose estate passed into the Bowes Lyon family in 1885, part of which is now National Trust property – Allen Banks.

The house was built of brick and stone rubble, rendered over with plaster and was spanned by a double ridged roof. There were 13 main rooms and bedrooms, also servants' quarters, offices and work rooms. In the entrance hall, was a full length mirror, opposite the front door, so that you 'met yourself' coming in. To the right of the hallway was the drawing room, lit by a large Venetian window, this being the grandest room in the house. One of the rooms was known as the School Room. In the back passage, was a bell system, to call servants from various rooms and also at the back, was a spiral stairway for the servants.

John Fryer, land surveyor, lived for a short while at Bird Hill. He was one of the Commissioners for the enclosure of Blackburn Fell.

Mrs Jane Grahamsley, a widow of independent means, was the tenant in the 1850s. Her companion was Jane Kirkley, daughter of Joseph Kirkley, who was the schoolmaster at Fellside in the 1820s. John, 10th Earl of Strathmore, bequeathed an endowment of £10 annually to the school. Mrs Grahamsley employed a cook, housemaid, coachman and a gardener.

In 1871, John Bush, a Newcastle solicitor, was at Bird Hill and in 1876, Archibald McIntyre, Clothier and Woolen Draper of Grainger Street, Newcastle, came here with his family.

The Winter family, who were connected with the iron and steel trade, lived at Bird Hill from 1906-1958. William Winter (1853-1936) is thought to have made corrugated sheeting for farm biers etc. Their children, Sidney, Violet and Fred, were the last tenants to occupy Bird Hill House. In 1958, when Sid Winter died, the house still had no mains water supply, or electricity and was in a dilapidated condition. It was condemned as unsafe and demolished by Alec Watson in 1962.

Bird Hill House.

The Woodmans Arms and the Watsons

The 'Woodmans' was lit by Tilly lamps which hung from the ceiling and heated by open coal fires. On Monday morning, 1st February 1926, a fire completely gutted the public house, with damage estimated at £3,000. Mr Alex Watson had only recently bought the place from the Strathmore estate. Alex and his wife

The east side of the Woodmans Arms, *circa* 1940.

Emma came to the Woodmans in 1924. The pub comprised of a bar, sitting room with piano, back kitchen and four upstairs rooms. The family lived in the adjoining cottage and when Gateshead Borough Fire Brigade arrived at 6.45 am their main concern was in protecting this cottage from damage, the pub by this time being well ablaze. Neighbours helped to remove furniture out on to the front garden. All that was retrieved from the pub after the fire was a safe and two barrels of beer in the cellar. A cottage adjoined the pub on the west and here the Thompson family lived in the late 1920s. Following the death of Alex, Emma sold the pub in 1948, but continued serving behind the bar, this time at the Causey Arch (up until the early 1960s), where her son Douglas was the

manager. Emma's other sons were Alec and Richard, both bricklayers. Ridley Milburn ran the Woodmans in the 1950s, his wife Dot waited on and Lily Hails played the piano. Emma died in 1970.

The Woodmans Arms has known many landlords and tenants over the years, it has also undergone many changes but local people will always remember Alex and Emma Watson.

This section of the Woodmans Arms is part of the original building viewed from the lane on the East side.

John English

John English (Lang Jack) came from Chester-le-Street to Winlaton Mill to work at the erection of the Chain Bridge at Scotswood in the year 1830. He was physically a giant, being 6ft 4ins in his stocking feet with a walking stride of 3ft 3ins, and remarkable for his great strength and endurance. He afterwards moved to the Woodhouse, near Whickham. In 1842, he erected the stone pillars for the bridge over the Derwent at Winlaton Mill. A stone on the bridge bears the inscription, 'John English, mason, Anno 1842.' He had apparently worked on the Newcastle Gaol and on St Thomas' Church at Barras Bridge.

He was known locally as 'The Tyneside Samson', a well earned title. Many stories are told of his extraordinary physical powers. Travellers by the Shotley Bridge turnpike are sure to have observed Jack's cottage, which he built on the west side of the highway between Whickham and Fellside.

JACK'S HOUSE. FELLSIDE

The stones of the house were quarried and drawn in a cart from the Woodhouse, a distance of a mile, by himself. Some pieces of stone of considerable size were carried from a quarry at Winlaton, nearly four miles distant. The chimney tops alone weighed almost twelve stones, he carried those unaided from Blaydon Quarry some four miles away, and dressed them himself. He was reputed to be ill-tempered. One day a cart filled with stones knocked over his dog and killed it. According to a friend, Jack was so annoyed that he took hold of the cart by a wheel and tipped the cart, complete with horse, down a bankside.

He wasn't the type of person one would invite home for a drink, he was reputed to have had an 'alcohol problem'. His 'party piece' was quite unusual. He would jump up and down on the spot each time getting higher and higher, until his head bumped the ceiling. It is known, that whilst performing his party piece at one house, the floor couldn't take his weight and collapsed underneath him. He ended up in a cowshed under the house and luckily unhurt.

He was very political and a familiar figure at the head of political processions. In one instance at the end of October 1831, a county demonstration was held at Durham, at which Mr Charles James Clavering, of Axwell Park, presided. Crowley's workmen accompanied by a Mr Attwood from Whickham attended the meeting. A rumour prevailed that the workmen at the pits of the Marquis of Londonderry would attend and attempt to break up the meeting. But Crowley's crew, with Lang Jack, as their leader, had armed themselves with 'peel-grains' or oak-saplings from Gibside wood, and waited around the platform for any hostile feeling that might be displayed by the pitmen. True enough, the pitmen began to manifest their disapproval of the utterances of one of the speakers. When Attwood called for Crowley's crew to preserve order, immediately the peel grains were wielded so effectively that the pitmen fled in disorder, and the meeting proceeded without further interruption. Crowley's men, after the meeting, were regaled with bread, cheese, and ale, after which they returned to Whickham and Swalwell.

A monument, erected in 1854, stood near the cottage. The figure of Jack was considered to be an excellent one. It was designed and executed by John Norvel of Swalwell. Crowds of people collected to see the monument unveiled. After the ceremony, a demonstration, headed by the Whickham Brass Band, marched to the Three Tuns Inn at Whickham, where speeches were made amidst great enthusiasm. Unfortunately, Jack gradually eroded his legendary strength and destroyed his once splendid constitution.

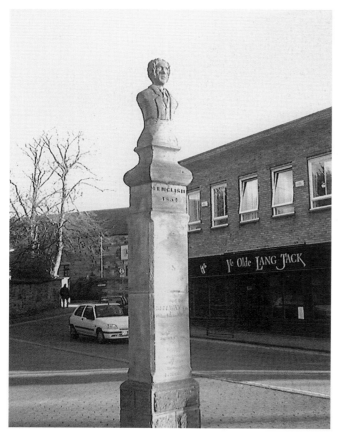

At his death on 26th August 1860 the cottage he built became the property of the Claverings, of Axwell, on whose land it stood.

His cottage was destroyed by a fire in 1907, the bust, which had stood next to it became vandalised. In 1976 Bellway builder moved and restored it to its present position in Whickham near the Crown Inn, a fitting memorial to an extraordinary character. In 1999 the Crown Inn closed for renovation and expansion work. In June 1999 it reopened with the name, 'Ye Olde Lang Jack'.

Jack's Monument at Ye Olde Lang Jack.

MARLEY HILL

F. Harrison, a Marley Hill miner.

Early Education

In the late eighteenth and nineteenth centuries Marley Hill Colliery was a thriving coal business with quite a large community living around the pit head. A school, built by the church before the parish was separated from Lamesley Parish, was built in the pit yard. The date of opening is unknown but in January 1779 there was an advertisement for a school master in the *Newcastle Journal* and the census of 1851 notes that a school mistress lived in Sandygate.

A class of the new Board School in the 1890s.

Fortunately the school log book dating from 1870 is in existence and it gives detailed recording of the life of Marley Hill Colliery National School, as it was then known. The school master was Mr Philip Blackman who lived in Sandygate and it seems to have been a boys' school because girls are not mentioned until August 1871. Other school masters mentioned are Mr W.S. Telford (1875-77) Mr I. Coates (1870-80) Mr N.G Maguire (1880-1882) Mr W. Franklin (1882-4) and Mr Lawrence Dewhurst who was appointed in October 1884.

In 1893 a site for a new school was selected to meet the needs of an ever increasing community, the new school was opened in 1895.

There have been seven head teachers:

Mr Dewhurst 1895-1913   Mr Bellerby 1913-45
Mr Atkinson 1947-65   Mr Gardner 1965-71
Mr Sykes 1971-91   Mr Rowland 1991-98
Mrs Westgarth 1998-present

One teacher's name lives on, Miss Thirlaway (infant class) gave her name to Thirlaway Terrace.

Marley Hill Council School, 1st Class, 1914.

Marley Hill Juniors, 1930. Back row: Mr Bellerby, Edward Shorten, William Allen, John Kindred, John Milburn, Robert Hinds, G. Robinson, Herbert Allsop, David Houliston, Robert Davison and Dennis Connelly. Middle row: Jenny Barker, Mary Pinkney, Jean Liddle, Gladys Prinn, Rita Davison, Jenny Wales, Eva Gooch, the Prinn twins, Nelly Vickery and Alice Carter. Front row: James Warnaby, Jack Morton, Kenneth Prinn, Steve Melton, Edward Morton, Alan Craig, Robert Ellison and Thomas Lawson.

A class at Marley Hill School with Mr William Bell on the right. Headmaster Mr John Atkinson is on the left.

William (Bill) Bell began his teaching career at Delves Lane County School. He moved to Marley Hill after the Second World War and stayed for ten years to become deputy headteacher, before moving on to a headship at Neasham County School (near Darlington) at the beginning of 1957. Subsequently he became headteacher of Pickering Nook County School and finally he became head of Catchgate County Primary School. Here he stayed until retirement in 1979.

The school held a variety of activities over the years, there were choir competitions, school sports days, inter school sports day and dance teams. Pictured opposite are just two of the teams 52 years ago.

With Apologies to Milton:

When I consider how my life is spent,
Ere half my days in school at Marley Hill
With boys and girls whom I attempt to fill
With knowledge; though full of good intent
To teach them quite enough, in case they're sent
Into the world unlearned, where it goes ill
With those whose aptitude is nil,
I grow depressed. But patience to prevent
Insanity soon replies. What you need
Is a big fat stick. That will make them try
To learn their poems and their sums. Be wild
When they you disobey, your warnings do not heed!
Beware their tears; crocodiles also cry.
He who spares the rod, also spoils the child.

By William Bell, Marley Hill School teacher, 1946-56

Marley Hill School Girls' Senior Dance Team, July 1950. Including: Frances Gaul, Dorothy Cawthorn, the Swinburn sisters, Nancy Finlay and Joan Douglas.

Marley Hill School Girls' Junior Dance Team, July 1950. Mary Fairlamb is front left and Margery McKie front right.

Marley Hill School, in its centenary year, 1995. The centenary in 1995 was a major event with community involvement and a chance for old pupils to meet again. It was a particularly happy occasion thanks to a lot of hard work by the teaching and administrative staff. This photograph taken at that time will bring back a lot of memories

Marley Hill Pit
'In Times of Struggle'

In February 1844 the miners at Marley Hill faced a reduction in wages due to a slump in the coal trade. Nicholas Wood of Killingworth, the agent, said that it was regrettable but necessary. The miners, already hard pressed to make ends meet, disagreed with him and went on strike. The Busty Seam was being wrought by fifty two hewers at the time.

Marley Hill Pit south side.

In addition to the wages, the miners were unhappy with the fines incurred on them – ie three pence fine for two quarts of stone, foul coal, or brass found in a tub, and six pence fine for four quarts. They argued that because of the tender nature of the coal it was difficult to pick out the stone waste by the light of a candle. The miners got the owners to buy a new weighing machine and a check weighman began to be employed by the miners to ensure fairness.

In April 1844 most of the Durham miners were on strike on similar grievances as the Marley Hill men – more convenient payment of wages, a fairer system of weighing, better inspection of mines, and renewal terms of the yearly bond. The latter was done away in 1872 and the principle of arbitration was introduced.

In 1847 John Bowes and Partners was formed when Charles M. Palmer joined the business. He had a sawmill and wagon works at Dunston.

Messrs Bowes and Partners worked both, under a term of sixty years beginning in 1846. The annual rent for the Marley Hill royalty was £700, and for Blackburn Fell, £550.

The partnership for the Colliery Company and the Coke Company at Marley Hill were each divided into twenty four shares.

The Marley Hill Colliery Company sold to the Marley Hill Coking Company all the coal necessary for the consumption of the coke ovens at nine shillings per chaldron at the pit.

William Potts in the winder house, *circa* 1916.

December 1849 saw the beginning of a short but very bitter dispute between the owners of Marley Hill Colliery and their workmen over low wages. The men were only able to earn between two shillings and sixpence, and three shillings and sixpence per day, and out of this they had to pay for shot firing powder, candles, and the repair of their tools. When they signed their yearly bond they expected to get about four shillings per day. The miners wanted the dispute to go to arbitration but the owners were unwilling to see this happen as they thought the workmen were dictating terms.

Without any warning several score of families were turned out of their homes and their goods carted away and dumped on Burdon Moor. Notices were displayed saying that those who had been ejected and sent adrift would be liable for trespass if they were found again on land belonging to the coal company.

Clockburn Drift entrance, opened in the 1950s.

The next step in the dispute was the arrival of forty-five workmen and their families, brought from Coatbridge in Scotland by the colliery owners. The men had not been told that a strike at the pit was in progress. To tempt them to break the strike the Scotsmen were offered significantly better terms than the Marley Hill men.

But sensing the mood of the local community and the striking miners, only about a dozen men decided to stay and work, the rest went back home or got work in nearby pits.

This introduction of the detested 'scab' (none Trade Union) labour led to the rest of the miners going on strike, which in turn led to an explosion at the Hobson Pit. On 11th January 1850 at 10 pm fifteen men in disguise approached the pit boilers. Damp coals were then thrown on the fires and a cask of gunpowder laid on the coals. When it exploded, the boilers were put out of action and work underground was suspended, this being the desired aim of the men who carried out the explosion.

Hobson Colliery had been supplying Marley Hill coke ovens with small coal during the strike but with the Hobson out of action, coke production almost ceased, which was a serious financial blow to the owners.

A reward notice was displayed at Marley Hill Colliery office stating that £50 would be given by the company to anyone giving information leading to the conviction of those persons responsible for the damage at the Hobson. No one claimed the reward.

In 1912 Marley Hill Miners' Trade Union Lodge had 308 members. The coal owners greediness and ill-treatment of the miners had ensured 100% trade union membership across the coalfields.

During the 1926 Coal Strike it was agreed between the union (union officials had a cabin in the pit yard) and management that a horse keeper could feed the ponies which had been left underground in the pit. There were 150 ponies and some were led underground along to Byermoor Colliery, taken up on bank, and stabled in the disused beehive coke ovens. Others were brought to bank at Marley Hill and kept in the field between Fenhouse and the school.

In 1953 Marley Hill Colliery saw some important developments which helped to ensure its future for a further thirty years. It was decided to work the Brockwell and Tilley Seams beneath Hollinside and Gibside from Marley Hill via a new drift at Clockburn (*opposite*). Axwell Park Colliery closed shortly after.

We already know that like all coal mines in the area, and indeed across Britain, Marley Hill pit was doomed. During the Thatcher Government's persecution of the coal miners, Marley Hill pit closed in March 1983.

Arthur Melton and Steve Ismay on the Rolleyway.

The Causey Arch

Sometimes called Tanfield Bridge or Dawson's Bridge, it was financed by Wortley and Liddell to carry the Tanfield Waggonway, from Thomas Dawson's Causey and Tanfield Collieries and ultimately to Dunston Staithes. It spans the Houghwell burn, which in the course of its wanderings becomes the Causey burn, the Beamish burn, then the River Team which flows into the

An artist's impression of coal chaldrons crossing the arch.

Tyne. The line came into operation in July 1725, but this bridge made of timber and built by Ralph Wood, collapsed and a second bridge was begun in August 1725 which took more than a year to erect. There was a sundial placed on top of the bridge, with the inscription, 'Ra. Wood Mason 1727'. Ralph Wood was a Master Mason commissioned by the Grand Allies, even though the first bridge collapsed he was allowed to begin the second.

In 1789 John Brand wrote an article about the bridge, in which he stated, 'The architect involved himself in many difficulties concerning it, and is reported to have committed suicide, because he thought the second bridge, like the first, would collapse.' Experts who have examined the structure conclude that his fears were groundless, there was never any likelihood that the arch would collapse. There is no documentation to support the suicide theory, quite often tales of suicide were attached to major buildings and it is unlikely that anyone will ever learn the truth. The cost was shared equally between Bowes, Liddell and the Wortleys (known as the Grand Alliance). There is an itemised bill showing various payments for the period 26th August 1725 to 5th November 1726 (see list opposite). For some reason Ralph Wood gave up the work in 1726, and H. Boag (1696-1763) replaced him. The bridge has a span of 105ft, it stands full 80ft above the stream, is 22ft x 7.5ins

The Causey Arch viewed from the valley.

wide on the soffit (underside of the arch) and is built of freestone. The embankments are restrained by massive walls, and a lot of work has been done to make the structure safe. The bridge road was originally drained by a series of stone trough like gargoyles which gradually became the home of birds nests. People from all over the world come to view, what is the earliest railway bridge in the world.

Copy of itemised payments	£	s	d
To R. Wood who undertook to build	1	1	0
Workmen's wages 26/8/1725 to 5/11/1726	907	0	0
Timber before 1/11/1726	197	12	10
To Hugh Boag 9/7/1726 to 5/11/1726	747	18	$3^1/2$
For lime and loading of same	12	18	0
For rag from Charles Atkinson	20	15	0
For oak timber to Thomas Surtees	12	15	$0^1/4$
To H. Boag, Geo Airey & Mr Davison	21	0	0
Inspection & care of the bridge	10	0	0
To R. Wood	15	15	0
At a total cost of	1946	15	$1^3/4$

A coal chaldron made of timber by modern day craftsmen. An exact copy of an original stands at the end of the arch.

Marley Hill Aged Miners' Homes

Members of Marley Hill Lodge of the Durham Miners' Association began to pay a penny a week in July 1929 to fund a scheme for building aged mine workers' homes at Marley Hill. The original plan was to build only four homes but this number was later increased to eight.

The stone laying ceremony was held on 9th May 1936. The Marley Hill Silver Prize Band led the procession from Sunniside up to the site and then the band accompanied the hymn singing. Speeches were made, followed by a public tea in the Welfare Hall.

A subsidy of £640 (£80 per home) was forthcoming from the Government in the form of the Commissioner for Special Areas. Messrs Bowes and Partners supplied the material at cost price and then further reduced the price by £100. They also granted the site at a nominal rent.

The homes were officially opened 22nd May 1937 by Major E.H. Kirkup, agent for Bowes and Partners, who deputised for Lord Glamis on this occasion. Mrs Crawford presented the keys to the first occupants, all married couples, who were to live there rent free and have free coals. Harry Bates, Dick Clifton, Joe Curry, Ben Porter, Bob Davidson, Tom Craig, Jack Musgrove and George Nicholson were the first retired miners to live there.

After the opening ceremony the company filed into the Welfare Hall to hear some speeches. Alec Crawford, chairman of the local committee of the Durham Aged Miners' Homes Association (DAMHA) said that there was some criticism of the choice of site as it overlooked the church yard and that the old folk would not like to be reminded of life's final journey. Alec rather wittily said that on one side there stood the Welfare, while on the other, the farewell, but in

Marley Hill people gather for the official opening of the Aged Miners' Homes.

The dignitaries accompanied by Reverend Probert of Marley Hill.

between were the homes, a constant reminder of a useful way in which to help retired folk.

It was pointed out that the success of the venture was due to the collective effort of many people. Other guest speakers included: Jack Lawson MP (for Chester-le-Street), Mr G. French (Secretary of the Durham Miners Deputies' Association), Mr W.S. Hall (Secretary of Durham Mechanics' Association), the Rev P.D. Beckwith (Methodist Minister), Rev Father Pickering of Byermoor and Mr A. Hetherington, the Colliery Manager. Also present were the officials of the DAMHA: Mr A. Mcdonald (Hon Treasurer), John Adair (Secretary) and the President William Whiteley, MP for Blaydon.

The names on the foundation stones somewhat reflect the social structure of the village at that time, the colliery officials, representatives of the Labour Party, the Co-operative Society, the church, the social club, farmers and businessmen.

Mention may be made of Councillor Alec Crawford (1894-1979). He served on Whickham Council during the 1930s, first as a Labour representative and then as an Independent. It seems he came from Bamburgh when he was eighteen and first stayed with the Berrys at Wasting Row. In 1925 he lived at Prospect Terrace and was a miner at Marley Hill Pit. He represented Whickham area on the Gateshead Board of Guardians. In 1934 he was chairman of the Marley Hill Lodge of the DMA and lived at Cuthbert Street with his family. In 1937 he was secretary of Marley Hill Branch of the Northumberland and Durham Miners' Permanent Relief Fund. Alec became a deputy overman and was elected secretary of Durham Miners' Deputies Association. He retired to Prinn Place and then on to Sunhill.

Also worthy of mention is the Kirkup family, some of whom made their mark in the coal industry. Philip Kirkup (1831-1911) farmed Urpeth Riding in the late nineteenth century and before that he farmed at Pelton. His eldest son

George took over at Urpeth Riding and was assistant overseer and collector at Kibblesworth for the Guardians of the Poor. His second son, Septimus, was a butcher and farmed East and South Farms at Kibblesworth. Two of his other sons, Fred and Austin, both trained as mining engineers. In 1906 Fred was manager of High Spen Colliery and a local magistrate, residing at Beda Lodge. From 1914-34 he lived at the Manor House, Medomsley and was the chief agent for the collieries of Consett Iron Company. Austin lived at the Manor House, Penshaw in 1906 and was agent to the Lambton Collieries. He retired to Morton Grange as agent to Lambton, Hetton, and Joicey Collieries Ltd. Another son, Thomas, was a Wesleyan minister.

Major E.H. Kirkup officially opening the first home.

Philip's nephew, Major E.H. Kirkup JP, was agent to Pelaw Main Collieries in the 1920s. He was agent to the Strathmore Estates 1937-1966 and retired to Leazes Hall. His father was general manager of Birtley Iron Company and a mining engineer for Bowes and Partners from 1907-17. Philip Kirkup Jnr was mining engineer to Holmside and South Moor Collieries in the 1930s.

Officials at the opening – Major Kirkup is second from the left and Alec Crawford is in the centre.

Marley Hill Welfare Hall

Marley Hill Miners' Welfare Hall and Institute, now called the Community Centre, was built around 1932 by Shield Brothers of Swalwell and replaced the old institute and reading room at Post Office Row. The miners paid about two pence a week into the welfare fund and with the money that was accumulated it had been debated whether to use it in building a welfare hall or a place where the miners could have a hot shower after a day's work.

The spacious hall was officially opened on 29th July 1936 by their Royal Highnesses the Duke and Duchess of York (the future George VI and Queen Elizabeth, the Queen Mother). Earlier on the same day they had met Lord Glamis the Duchess' brother and opened the Glamis Pit of which he was chairman. They also donned overalls and went underground to view the workings. The Duke and Duchess also opened a welfare hall at Kibblesworth and then travelled on to Gibside, ancestral home of the Duchess, to visit the chapel and speak to estate workers.

Mr J. Clark of Glamis Terrace was the first secretary of the new Welfare Hall and in 1935 William Anderson of Cresta, High Byermoor, the colliery engineer, took over this appointment.

In the 1930s the Welfare held dances on Saturday nights. There was a billiard room and reading room upstairs. The Marley Hill branch of the Women's Institute, formed in 1929, and met here soon after the hall opened. They still meet here once a month. Durham County Library rented a room in 1937 and a maternity and child welfare centre was set up by Whickham Council. Marley Hill Boys' Club had a new hut built in 1936 beside the colliery offices. Joe Young was one of the leaders. Five years later the Boys' Club met at the Welfare Hall and also at the cricket pavilion. Ruth Anderson, a teacher at Byermoor, ran the club in conjunction with the Girls' Training Corps. The boys formed a football team and for a few years played in the Stanley and District Youth League.

Marley Hill carpet bowls began in 1982 when the equipment was on loan from the Bowburn Club. Within six months the Marley Hill players were able to buy their own carpet, bowls and centre piece with a donation from Marley Hill Colliery. In 1984 a second carpet was acquired by a donation from Gateshead Council and £150 from the club's own funds.

The season 1985-6 saw the club promoted to division one in

The Duchess of York playing bowls.

the North-west Durham Carpet Bowls League. Jack Morton took over from Rob Carlton as treasurer, Billy McKie became chairman when Arthur Melton stepped down, and Chris Caisley stayed on as secretary. In 1991 a third carpet was bought with a donation from the Community Centre Committee. The club began with a dozen members and numbers rose to 33 in the early 1990s.

The Ladies' darts team met every Thursday night and had a dozen members. Ruth Soulsby began the club in 1978 at the over 60s Hall at Sunniside and moved to the Community Centre in 1982. The Modem Sequence Dance Club met on Wednesday evenings and had about 70 members.

The Bright Sparks formed in 1988, occasionally performed here in aid of charity. Thousands of pounds have been raised for the Madame Curie Institute, McMillan Nurses, and to help people with Multiple Sclerosis and Motor Neurone Disease. The performers gave their time and energy for free and they made up their own costumes. Local support was strong. The singers were: George Bright, Fred Rocket, Ted Young, Nell Armstrong, Edna Brown, Phyllis Tulip, Joan Heron and Ruth Soulsby. Dancers and singers were: Tess Larmour, Cathy Caisley, Nancy Mudd and Betty Williams. Musical accompaniment was by Joe Thompson (piano) Davy Mudd and Davy Larmour (harmonica) and George Rowell (trumpet). The Bright Sparks disbanded in 2001.

The Centre still boasts a very busy and wide range of activities, including: bingo, indoor bowls, mother and toddler group, badminton, line dancing, dog training, monthly dance, and the Marron School of Dancing run by Mrs Vicki Richardson. Standards at the school are very high and the pupils have appeared in pantomime with some very famous names in venues such as Theatre Royal Newcastle.

Councillor Alan Ord feels that the Welfare Hall, although now named the Community Centre, will always live in the hearts of the community as a great memorial to the coal miners.

The first committee of the Welfare Hall, 1936. Back row: Charles Meddick, Will Marshal, Tom Hogg, Ernest Cooper, George Johnson and Billy Dent. Front row: Jack Adair, Tom Gilliland, Alec Crawford, Jack Cape and Heath Hodgson.

The Welfare Hall/Community Centre.

The Bright Sparks

The Bright Sparks, formed in 1988, occasionally performed at the Welfare Hall in aid of charity. Gradually, the years took their toll and eventually the Bright Sparks retired but their achievements in fund raising for charity were immense and very commendable. *Above*: On a fund raising night, left to right: Ruth Soulsby, Phyliss Tulip, Tess Larmour, David (Tuppy) Larmour, Nancy Mudd, Joan Heron, Nell Armstrong, Kath Caisley, Edna Brown and Fred Rockett.

Marley Hill Cricket

Taking the road from High Marley Hill to Sunniside and down a steepish bank, sometimes called Berkley's Bank, which levels out to the junction with the lane to Longfield House, on the right was the recreation field, used from 1925-46. Prior to this the sports field was next to the cokeworks but this site was abandoned when the acid plant was built.

A cricket club was formed in 1881 at Marley Hill and continued up till the Second World War. The late 1920s was the most successful period for the club when it played in the North Durham Senior League. It was admitted into this league in 1923 after winning the Tyne and District League the previous season. In 1927 they were league champions and won the Whickham Nursing Cup and the Elsey Cup. Some of the first team players: James Batey (captain), Les Hutchinson (wicketkeeper) who was invited to play a trial for Warwickshire CCC in 1931, brothers Billy and Jack Reed, Jack Wilson (who played as a half back for Manchester United), Ernie Spriggs, Jack Davison, Tom Liddle, J. Hogson, L. Parkin, I. Spoors, Phillipson, S. Morton, E. Morton, T. Morton, Billy Wintrip (who was invited for trials with Newcastle United) and R. Hickson. Fred Kendal was secretary of the club at this time. J.S. Nesbit and Pearson Sharp were influential club members in earlier years. There was also a very successful ladies' cricket team.

About 1946 the cricket pavilion was dismantled and re-erected for use as the bowling green hut, behind the Welfare Hall.

The 1940 Marley Hill Ladies' cricket club members.

Marley Hill Ladies' cricket team players, Joan Davison, Freda Kendall and Isa Marsham, 1940.

As a result of producing our two previous books I get many letters, these are generally from people who have either lived in the area or who have relatives still living here. I have included extracts from two such letters sent by cousins Thelma Nichols of Southend and Ruth Crossley of Lancashire, their family, the 'Potts', originated from Marley Hill.

Ruth's Story

On my mother's side (Isabella Potts), my grandfather (William Potts) was a winding engineman at either Burnopfield or Marley Hill Colliery. He was 70 when he died in 1936. He was a Methodist local preacher and the whole family worshipped at Burnopfield Methodist Church. They lived in a street just off the main road. I have forgotten the name but I visited many times. He was married to Katherine Ann (née Gray). She died in 1937 at my home in Wallsend. They are both buried in Marley Hill churchyard. They had four children, Ernest, Sarah, Isabel and Harold. Sarah married Billy Musgrave, there's a photo of him in your first book. Uncle Billy worked in the pit and at first they had one of the new houses in Marley Hill just above the graveyard. In later years Uncle Billy did not want anymore responsibility and so they had to move into a house on the front street of the main road, I think it was number 27. Dr Boland had a place in Aunty Sarah's large larder, he would come twice a week to make up medicines and see if anyone needed him to visit.

They had one daughter, Linda, who married Jackie Burridge from the Hobson. I would go with Linda to visit Jackie's family up Hobson Bank. In the Second World War Jackie was posted to Cyprus. He was away for three years and was absent at the birth of his daughter, Joyce, who now lives in Whickham, she is 60 now. Jackie and Linda lived in Burnopfield on the main road, No 9 Derwent View, they both died in the 1980s. Ernest married Eveline Thomas.

Isabella Potts (my mother) married George Young from Wallsend, previously from the Causey. She has one daughter, Ruth. They lived in Wallsend until 1965, then came to Manchester to live next to Ruth. They both died in 1978. Harold Potts married Jennie, they lived all their lives in Burnopfield at No 2 Poplar Terrace. Uncle Harold was the caretaker at the local school. During the war they ran the Co-optimists concert party with another couple Mr and Mrs Seth. They had no children and I am not sure when they died, it must have been in the 1980s. I often stayed with Aunty Sarah and Uncle Billy at Marley Hill when I was young. I went with Linda to the cinema in Burnopfield, but when we felt posh we would go to Stanley Picture House on a Friday evening. I would often buy myself a bag of carrots to eat in the cinema at Burnopfield – the Co-op was just next door if my memory serves me correctly. I loved carrots.

William Potts.

There were no pitbaths in those days at Marley Hill Colliery, so I would wait for Uncle Billy coming across the field. I could always see him from the top step outside the back door. He would be black and Aunty Sarah would have the water in the boiler ready for his bath. The kitchen door would be shut and I was never allowed near until he was finished. He would have his dinner and then off to bed.

On my dad's side, my grandfather was called Tom Young. He had two brothers Stephen and Jack. When young they lived at the Causey but they moved down to Wallsend when older. Grandad was a joiner and he got a good job in Wallsend and was 70 when he died in 1943. My grandmother was Susannah Rattery Chalmers, she would talk to me a lot about Andrews House and Causey Arch. She seemed to deliver all the babies and lay out the dead.

She terrified me by the stories of putting pennies on dead people's eyes and putting newly born babies who had died under the bed while she looked after the mums. She had a sister Mary, called Bainbridge when she married, and as far as I remember she stayed at the Causey – her husband was Joe Bainbridge. She also had a sister called Ann, she married either Tom or John Blackmore. I often went to Sunniside with Grandma to visit, they lived just around the corner from Sunniside Methodist Chapel. John or Tom had a sister on the main road near the Methodist Chapel, we went to visit her. Grandma also had a brother called Archie who worked down one of the pits. He was killed and was carried out of the pit on a door. Archie had married Annie and they had one son, George. I must be talking about the years 1940-50. Tom and Susannah lived in Wallsend all their lives after that, they had three children one of them being my father.

Thelma's Story

My father, Ernest Potts, was born in 1895 and died in 1982 aged 87 years. Dad went down Marley Hill pit aged 14 years to be a pony driver. He worked down the pit until 1914 then, when he was 18 years old, he joined the Royal Marines. He fought in France and at Gallipoli and was wounded in the neck. Unfortunately he contracted malaria and dysentery, both potentially fatal diseases and as a consequence, like so many other young men, was discharged from the forces.

He met and married my mother, Eveline Thomas, who was a Londoner. In 1922 he left Marley Hill to be with her, I was their only child. My father only returned there for two short visits, once when my Grandfather died in 1935 and again in 1946/7. When he first left Marley Hill unemployment was still a huge problem, so Dad 'jobbed about'. He eventually obtained full-time employment in a gasworks and stayed there until his retirement.

I had not visited my dad's home since 1940 when my mother and I went to stay with his brother Harold while our cities were being bombed during the Battle of Britain. But I went back on holiday and visited Beamish Museum. I also visited a colliery and was horrified at the conditions that men and children were made to work in. The mine owners must have been unfeeling greedy people or maybe they just didn't care as long as they were well off.

Ernest Potts (left) while serving in the Royal Marines.

Marley Hill Folk

Kate and William Potts with their daughter-in-law Eveline centre. Seated at the front is Thelma, the daughter of Eveline and Ernest Potts.

The wedding of David (Tuppy) Larmour to Elsie (Tess) Nicholson on 13th September 1947. Left to right, Bridesmaid Jean Forster, David, Elsie and Best Man Bob Forster. Tess was one of the founder members of the Bright Sparks concert party whilst Tuppy was a gifted cornet player in Marley Hill Colliery Band. Arguably the best player in the region he was also in big demand to join other brass bands.

Marley Hill Colliery Mechanics annual trip, 1951.

George and Elizabeth Ann
Hetherington (left) with Bart and
Ethel Casson (right), *circa* 1940s.

Meg Arnold with children Thomas
and Clara. Clara would eventually
marry Thomas White of Sunniside.

Churches do not seem to be at the centre of the community in this day and age and St Cuthbert's Church, Marley Hill is no exception. The community has shrunk since the closure of the colliery which has adversely affected the congregation attendance. These two photographs were taken in happier times when people were very much more involved with the church and fund raising. During the period of the Reverend Probert (1929-58), his wife was a fervent activist, she often stopped locals and pupils of Marley Hill School and chastised them for not going to church. At services she always sang with great gusto and could be heard over and above everyone else, she didn't hesitate to prompt or correct the Reverend Probert during a service if he inadvertently erred. Mrs Probert is pictured here on the left of both photographs wearing a flowery dress, while fund raising at the vicarage during a garden fete in the 1930s.

Hannah Williams pictured here around 1926 at her door in Colliery Houses, Marley Hill, with her son Ken who was born on 8th December 1923. The colliery rows were tied houses, the occupier or one of the family had to be employed by Bowes and Partners. No rent was paid but if circumstances changed and none of the occupiers worked for the company then they had to find other accommodation. Before the First World War the company tended to be benevolent towards their long serving workmen and when retirement came (the men usually retired in their 70s) some were given pensions and were not turned out on the street. Attitudes hardened after the war and the company issued eviction orders to sick, injured and elderly tenants of their property who were no longer able to work for them. Many a man went to work his shift when very ill, he was obliged to, because his family depended on him. The loss of the 'rent free' house hung like a dark cloud over many families and made the men totally subservient.

Mrs Nellie Davison (née Aimers) lived at Colliery Houses, Old Marley Hill, near the pit in her younger days. She described the living conditions as being greatly aggravated by the industry surrounding them, and literally on the doorstep. The coalmine on one end, the cokeworks at the other end, the tarworks and chemical plants below, and the railway line running alongside Coke Row. The houses were always very dusty with excessive levels of fumes and smells, some now known to be injurious to health. Noise levels were constant, twenty-four hours a day, from the mine and cokeworks, but worst of all from the shunting backward and forward of the railway engines and trucks. Throughout the night there was the noise of buffers clanging together, the roaring of the engine, the rumble of the coal trucks, and the men shouting to each other. Nellie and her family did not reside for long at Colliery Houses, they moved to the new houses facing the fields, not far from St Cuthbert's Church. She is pictured here in 1995 during the Marley Hill School Centenary celebrations as the oldest ex-pupil, at the age of 92 years, with the youngest current pupil, Jonathan Gilbert, aged four years.

SUNNISIDE

Sunniside Carnival Parade preparing to leave the side of the Travellers Rest Inn in the 1940s.

Granby Terrace & The Greyhound Inn

Following the formation of a turnpike trust in 1797, with powers to improve the Gateshead to Wolsingham road, a new route was chosen from between Streetgate to Maiden Law, which followed Sunniside, Marley Hill, High Marley Hill, then on to Crookgate, The Hobson, Flint Hill and Catchgate.

Robert Thirlaway (1759-1831), of Streetgate Lane, was allotted the acres where Granby, Thirlaway and Ravensworth Terraces now stand, also what was known as Snow's Field.

In 1841, William Thirlaway (1787-1845), began to build Granby Terrace, starting at the top end next to the Old Chapel. Chapel Opening, was at this time, very narrow, due to a coal shed abutting on the side of the chapel. The opening led to a garden at the back. This was before a lane was made, up to the top end of Ravensworth Terrace, in the late 1850s.

Colin Dobson with the Old Chapel, complete with wall, behind him.

William's eldest son, John Thirlaway (1824-1903), owned Granby Terrace in 1856, at which time, he was the victualler at the Granby Arms, Low Streetgate. John, along with his brother Thomas Grey Thirlaway (1827-1907), also ran Streetgate Farm.

The top end of Thirlaway Terrace, was built in the early 1890s, they were originally flats. Home Cottage is dated 1889. Between here and No 19 Granby Terrace, there was a short row of toilets and a pair of stone houses, which were back-to-back two by two in 1891. They were still standing in 1949. Towards the bottom end of Granby Terrace, the front of the houses were built with colliery firebricks, on the site known as 'The Wash Hole'.

Granby Terrace looking East.

There has been a shop, where the 'Pot Pourri' stands now, at No 5 Granby Terrace for many years. Tom Henderson (1817-1901), was a grocer here for 40 years, before he retired in 1894. He was also class leader and superintendent of the Sunday school at Sunniside. Tom worked at Marley Hill Coke Ovens, and his wife and daughter kept the shop. His daughter, Mary Ann, married Walter Fenton (1850-1920), of Lingy Fine. The shop became the post office in 1893, with Walter as the sub-postmaster, after a lapse of a few years, resumed again in 1904. Walter was a Sunday school teacher at Sunniside Methodist Chapel and served for a number of years on Chester-le-Street Rural District Council, Chester-le-Street Board of Guardians and Whickham School Board. Mary Fenton continued to run the post office, grocery and drapery shop after Walter's death.

No 14 was the last house to be built in the Terrace. Up until about 1860, there had been a gap in the Terrace here, to allow access to some of the rear yards. A narrow passage remained here and was used as a short cut from Holmside Terrace to the Front Street but this was blocked up in 1958.

The Terrace was built around 1905 for the Holmes family on land bought from Mr W. Snow. It overlooked Snow's Field which was home to 'Patch' a bay horse for many years. The field was built on in 1988. The path which leads from there to Lingy Fine is at least 155 years old and prior to the Enclosures was probably a Bridle Way.

Next door at No 15 Granby Terrace, Tom Crawford had a grocer's shop from 1850 to 1891. In the 1920s the Kehoe sisters, had a milliner's shop at No 17. Around 1900, Doctor Arthur William Attwater (1847-1904) of Whickham, held a surgery at No 7 Granby Terrace and in the early 1920s Mrs Burns, let her front room at No 8, to Dr Andrew Smith of Whickham.

A public beer house was built of stone around 1858, it was called The Greyhound. Robert Fenwick was the first licensee and he also worked as a cobbler. During the 1870s, Alexander Livingstone was the beer house keeper and he also had another job at Marley Hill Coke Ovens. In 1891, the house was called the Board, which was once a common name for a pub, and was ran by George Stott. Public houses showing no sign were commonly called the Board or sometimes the Letters. George had been a butcher at Streetgate, while his younger brother William, kept the Rose, Shamrock and Thistle, as well as being a butcher. By 1894, George had changed the name to the Traveller's Rest.

Above: Holmside Terrace prior to building Sun Hill Sheltered Accommodation in 1968.

Left: Snow's Field prior to buildings with 'Patch' and Andrew Batey

Granby Terrace looking west with the Greyhound Inn partially obscured by the larger building in the foreground. Over the years the pub was well attended, particularly on a Sunday morning when the Marley Hill Colliery Silver Prize Band practised in the back room. It was excellent entertainment for the customers who could listen to the band playing whilst drinking in the bar. On Durham Miners' Gala Day the band would form up at Marley Hill then march down to the front of the pub with union lodge officials, proudly carrying their banner.

Marley Hill Silver Prize Band, *circa* 1950.

They would play a few pieces before embarking for Durham City. During the 1930s through to the 1950s a carnival was held, starting at the side of the Travellers then marching off in procession, in the early years down to the field adjoining Streetgate Farm then changing to the football field at Marley Hill. Local people used to dress up in fancy dress and compete for prizes. All manner of events were held, mainly to entertain young people.

Sunniside Co-op

The first shop of Tanfield Industrial and Provident Co-op Society was established in a cottage at Causey Row. In the early 1860s it prospered and new premises were acquired within a few years at White-le-Head and, in 1866, new shops were built at Tantobie.

The Co-op did not arrive in Sunniside until fifty-three years after the first one in our area opened at Blaydon in 1867. The members in the Burnopfield area broke away to form Burnopfield Co-op Society in 1889.

Swalwell Co-op Society was established in 1864 and, although it opened a branch at Whickham Bank Top in 1910 and another at Broom Lane in 1934, it remained a comparatively small society. Some people in our area travelled to Burnopfield, Gateshead or Dunston Co-ops seeking better bargains.

In July 1911, Sunniside Branch of Burnopfield Co-op was opened in Dewhurst Terrace by Mr J.W. Bell, President of the Society. At Nos 1 and 2 Dewhurst were: grocery, drapery and butchery departments on the ground floor. Above were: billiard and reading rooms as well as a library. No 3 Dewhurst, became the manager's house. In September 1921, new premises, adjoining the top end of Dewhurst Terrace were opened by Mr Robert Heslop, President of Burnopfield Co-op Society. Built by Messrs A.&.R. Davis of Burnopfield, designed by John Eltringham of Blackhill. The carpentry, shop fixtures and central heating installation, were done by CWS workmen. The front was faced with freestone from Heworth Burn Quarry. Blythes of Birtley supplied most of the bricks, excluding the glazed bricks (for facing the flour warehouse and packing room walls).

The rear part of the grocery department was used for packing. There was also a loading dock with hoist alongside. This communicated with the flour and grain warehouse above. The flour and grain were conveyed by galvanised steel chutes, down to the packing room. A dry goods store-room, lit from the top, was next to the packing room. There was further storage in the lower ground floor.

Next door was the drapery department with a warehouse at the rear with access to the loading dock. A handsome staircase, with stained glass windows, led from the drapery to the millinery showroom and boot & shoe department.

At the rear of the premises were stables, harness room and a covered shed for vans. (Now being used by Lowdon's buses.) The total cost was around £13,600.

The butcher remained at No 2 Dewhurst Terrace and the greengrocers was begun at No 1. In the early 1920s, Tom Anderson was in charge of the two tables in the billiard room, later, in the early 1930s, Billy Cruddace took charge.

The hardware and shoe department had a staff of two, and

The Co-op, *circa* 1920.

Margaret Young was an assistant.

Mr R. Stonehouse was in charge of the grocery department, assisted by Frank Nichol and Cecil Kendal. He later went on rounds in a store van to Marley Hill, selling groceries and taking orders. Fred Armstrong and Janet Bell worked in the greengrocers. Tom Brabban and Mary Pattison also worked at the store. Around 1950, Mary McConnon came to work at Sunniside, shortly after the greengrocery moved into the main building and a chemist shop moved into No 1 Dewhurst Terrace, people still had to go to Whickham to get doctor's prescriptions. Joe Croft was the store butcher. The store's abattoir was behind Fell Terrace (owned by the Co-op), at the top of Crookbank, Burnopfield, known locally as Shield's Abattoir.

About five people worked in the grocery, two in the hardware, and two upstairs in the drapery. Mary went round the houses taking orders and a man from Gateshead Co-op did the same. Members of Gateshead had a better choice of goods and a better dividend. The 'divi' (as it was affectionately known) was paid out upstairs. In the early 1950s it was 2s 6d in the pound and paid quarterly, later it was paid half yearly. On divi day there was usually a sale, when shop soiled goods and lines not selling were disposed of. There was an Appro (on approval) Book, in which receipted slips were recorded for those taking items, such as shoes, on trial, but not yet paying for them. There was a Door Club, in which Co-op members were given credit, based on the amount of dividend they had in their books and whether they were reliable payers. For doorstep milk delivery, the Co-op operated a milk token system, different colours for various types of milk. The milk was bottled at the Annfield Plain Dairy.

The Sunniside Co-op experienced many changes over the years, but as part of a strategy by the Co-op movement to centralise operations at selected branches, the Sunniside Branch ceased trading in 1987. Thereafter the building changed hands as different ventures were tried.

The Co-op building as a saddlery and a Spar supermarket.

On the night of 12th March 1992, in the early hours of the morning, a fire broke out and destroyed the main part of the premises. It is strange that a building, which when it was built boasted 'metal fire proof ceilings', could burn down so quickly.

Above: Later in the day with fire appliances still in attendance.

Right: Fire appliances at the rear of the building, the stable was untouched.

All that remained of the original buildings were two shops, once the chemists and butchers.

Newspapers in Sunniside

In the early 1920s Jack 'Pet' Mason sold newspapers from his front door at No 16 Dewhurst Terrace. He went by horse and trap to collect the papers at Swalwell Station. He kept the pony in Snow's Field and also led small loads of coal and a bit of furniture removal, but only in a small way. His daughter Ethel helped him to deliver papers and she continued up to 1951.

In 1925 Tom Blackmore had a newsagents shop at No 9 Dewhurst Terrace and was assisted by his wife Ethel. In 1938 Mr Bundy ran the shop, Charlotte Rutherford did the paper round for 9 shillings a week. Charlotte walked from Wasting Row to get to the shop by 6.00 am and delivered to the Crescent first of all. She then came back to the shop to pick up the papers for Peters Gates, Andrews House, the Causey, Beamish Red Row, and most of the farms on the way. She got back home on a good day by 9.30 am. The afternoon round began at 3.30 pm. She then delivered to the Council Houses, Whickham Road, Hole Lane, Streetgate and Pennyfine Road. Charlotte usually finished by 5.00 pm but if the papers came into the shop late, or when the winter snow fell, then it meant a later finish.

In 1921, Harry Ord had a Drug Store at No 12 and by 1929 William and Sydney Blackburn had taken it over. The shop became a newsagents in 1952, when Thomas (Tommy) White established the business.

In his younger days, Tommy was an apprentice joiner to Dick Clarke of Streetgate for a few years. The better wages were to be made at Marley Hill Colliery and this lured him away before completing his apprenticeship. When Tom died in 1970 the business was continued by his daughter Margery, and his son Andrew (Andy). It was then the oldest family shop in Sunniside. The shop has now passed from the hands of the White family.

The White family lived at the bottom of Beech Street from the 1940s to '60s. During the war years and after, Mrs Clara White was extremely kind and helpful to families who were facing hard times. Mrs White died in 1986, she was truly a lovely lady.

Tommy White with his son Andy.

Margery and Andy White, *circa* 1947.

Mrs Clara White.

White Elephant School From Beginning To End

The school was built in 1913 at a cost of £700 on a site granted by Lord Ravensworth. It was made of timber, with latted walls rendered in pebble dash. The building started out as a Mission Hall for St Cuthbert's Church, Marley Hill, and during part of the First World War, soldiers were billeted there. In the 1920s, the Marley Hill Company of the Church Lads Brigade (Kings Royal Rifles) trained in the hall. Captain Bertie Dent MC was leader of the company in 1922, as a Lieutenant in the 10th Northumberland Fusiliers, he won the Military Cross for gallantry when fighting in France. His elder brother, Corporal T.S. Dent, was killed in action in France in September 1916. Their father, Mr Thomas Dent, was the manager of the Coke Ovens at Marley Hill in the 1890s. Bertie was a clerk at the new cokeworks after the Great War ended, and in 1925 he lived at 'Hillcrest', Streetgate. He served as an Army major in the Second World War. Each month the company attended church parade in full uniform at Marley Hill, this was as well as each Armistice Sunday.

The story of the building as Sunniside Infant School really begins in August 1907 when a Miss Jackson was appointed headmistress of an infant department within Marley Hill Colliery School. This school continued to function with the appointment of Miss Hannah Armstrong as headteacher on 1st November 1921, until 1923. Then the number of children attending the school was so great, it was decided to open a temporary infant school in Sunniside. It was recorded in Marley Hill Infant School log book: 'April 20th 1923, Hannah Armstrong, headteacher, Lesley Cuthbert CA and Ethel Smith PT finish duty today and will commence on the 23rd at Sunniside Temporary Council School. The Sunniside children have been transferred to the temporary school, the other children remain here as an infant class of the mixed department.'

The school opened on 23rd April 1923, by then it consisted of an 'L' shaped hall with a stage. It was rented to Durham Authority at a 'peppercorn' rent of

This is a photograph of a class at the White Elephant School, *circa* 1920 – it is probably the oldest one in existence. The group is almost certainly not just a class but every child in the school. Unusually there are no teachers present.

1 shilling per annum. A temporary action to fulfil a need – to last forty years. The school enjoyed a very stable staff with only three head teachers during its life-time. Miss Hannah Armstrong belonged to Blackhall Mill where she had a niece, but lodged with a Mrs Bell in Sun Street.

Miss Lesley Cuthbert lived at Lobley Hill, she joined the staff of Marley Hill Infant School in 1911 as a newly qualified class assistant and as already stated, was moved with Miss Armstrong to Sunniside in 1923. Miss Cuthbert became head in 1948 on the retirement of Miss Armstrong and retired herself in 1951, after 40 years service teaching children of this area. Miss Cuthbert was a gentle, soft-spoken lady. She played the violin beautifully and supplied the music at school assembly. Miss Cuthbert played by ear and never seemed to need to read a music score.

Miss Mabel Davison was the other head who was appointed in 1951 on the retirement of Miss Cuthbert. Miss Davison left in December 1962 after eleven years and Mrs A. Grant was acting head until the school finally closed in 1963.

After closure the building stood idle and then it was sold by the church on the 25th November 1965 to the Dumighan Brothers. They tried to develop it and were refused planning permission. It was then sold to Mr McLennan, a heating engineer, who used it as a depot/warehouse. It was burnt to the ground in a spectacular fire on 7th March 1975. Eventually Mr Harry Brown bought the site and built a bungalow 'High Trees' in 1984.

Class photographs appear once in a while. The one featured, *circa* 1952, was loaned by Mr Joe Tate, formerly of Old Sunniside Farm. Back row: Sandra Burns, Victoria Dillon, Mary Ibbetson, Harold Harrison, Ronald Taylor, John Caisley, Atholl Campbell, Arthur Scorer, Joseph Tate and Sylvia Wallace. Middle row: Peter Amos, Edward Clapperton, David Armstrong, George Elliott, Robert Steele, Derek Morton, John Burnip and Miss Mabel Davison. Front row: Dorothy Ibbetson, Steven Chisholm, Gwynneth Debie, Dorothy Thompson, Joyce Ellis, Carol Appleby, Christine Reay, Maureen Palmer, Ann Hyland and William Alfred.

Our Village People

Years ago a lot of the social life in the villages centred around the pubs and clubs, there was very little else to do. Saturday and Sunday mornings at the pubs and clubs were an occasion for the men to get together socially after a hard week's work, especially the coal miners. The conversation very rarely varied. The pitmen loved to talk about work and they took a great pride in what they did. Looking around the bar you could see arms waving as though they were hewing coal or knocking in props. Having a drinking session with a pitmen was like working a shift, you left the bar worn out, but they were great men, very courageous and very generous. Outside of work people were inventive when it came to entertainment. There were church organised functions, trips to the seaside and street parties on special occasions, how many of us remember the Victory party following the Second World War or the Coronation party? There was carnivals, sports days, flower shows and it seemed that it was the women who were the most active, they were the driving force behind most organisations and ventures. Who can forget those very 'Jolly Girls' of Sunniside Club, the 'Over Sixties', the various Concert Parties and of course the Women's Institute, one of the few organisations to survive? The pubs and clubs did their part too, organising summer trips for the kids, Christmas parties for the children and old people – all designed to maintain and foster a community spirit. While a few traditions still remain, it is a matter of great regret that the community spirit of old is generally no longer with us. I hope, however, that the following photographs may bring back memories of those happier days.

One exception to the demise of so many worthy organisations is the thriving and popular Sunniside and District Local History Society who meet monthly at Sunniside Social Club. The society holds all the values of a successful organisation dear, especially friendship and interesting activities. Pictured above during a society visit to Harewood House is our Treasurer Sheila Gascoigne (on the left) and Secretary Eleanor Baty, typifying a relaxing and enjoyable day out. We are immensely pleased and proud that our books have given so much pleasure to so many people, especially those who are now 'far from home'.

Local lads on holiday, right to left: Tony Phelps, Stewart Orwin, Jack Porter, Derek Best, Jimmy Eltringham and Harvey Boland. Sadly Tony, Stewart and Harvey did not enjoy a long life, but whilst with us they had a great capacity for enjoying themselves.

A night out at Sunniside Club. Right to left: Frances Clifton, Ella Herries, Tommy Herries, Magdalen Graham, Hilda Skeen (the Gracie Fields of Sunniside) and Mary Orwin.

The Sunniside Club Jolly Girls on stage, among others are: Mary Robinson the Club Stewardess, Ma Barron, Ella Herries, Lizzie Orwin and Mary Orwin.

A group of Jolly Girls on holiday, among others: Mary Orwin, Ma Barron, Mary Robinson, Rhia Liddle, Francis Clifton and Evelyn Callaghan.

A party at the Over Sixties Hall, Sunniside. The man with the bow tie is John O'Neill, he was a former manager of Sunniside Co-op and a Labour Party Councillor on Whickham Urban District Council.

Sunniside ladies, Jean Coyle, Hilda Clifton, Lily Bell and Jenny Elliott.

It is the Queen's Golden Jubilee this year of 2002, in 1953 the folks of the Sunniside Council houses collected money and held a party to celebrate the Queen's Coronation. Because of the awful weather the party was held in Tates new barn at Old Sunniside Farm.

These photographs were taken at the barn entrance during the festivities. From left to right: Angus Newman, Gerald Boland, Roland Ibbetson, Iris Smith, Polly Vickery, Francis G. Newman, Harvey Boland, Joan Boyd, Bobby Boyd, Raymond Gilhespie with a young Billy Boyd.

It is difficult to recall all names but among those present are: Sheila and Betty Cant, Queenie Nelson, Honor Boyd, Roland Ibettson, Iris Smith, Maureen Mitchell, Margaret Boyd, Alma Newman and Helen Murray. Sincere apologies to those unnamed.

It may well be that sisters Gwyneth and Madeleine Debie will not thank me for including this photograph, but I think that they pose so gracefully it is worthy of inclusion. I will not venture to hazard a guess at the date.

A group of friends meet up during the Second World War to celebrate Ivy Todd's 21st Birthday. Standing: Fred (surname unknown), Ivy Todd, Eddie Rose. Seated: Rita Todd and Doris Dinning. Ivy was on leave from the ATS.

At 'Sans Souci', No 53 Sunniside, Lawrence Dewhurst is pictured with his wife Miriam and two of his daughters. He spent his retirement here from 1913 until his death in 1926, at the age of 75. He was headmaster of Marley Hill National School, 1883-95.

Cuthy Bell and Tom Davison pictured here during the 1950s snow clearing on Elm Street.

Sunniside Methodist Chapel is very much at the centre of the community. The activists take the time and trouble to organise various events as a means of drawing the community together outside of the Chapel as well as inside. Shown here on a day excursion at the seaside some years ago are among others, Margaret and Wilfred Craig, Jack and Joyce Stoneman.

The Over Sixties Club of years ago was very well attended and organised, shown here on an excursion are a group of the members in June 1967. Third from the right on the front row is John O'Neill, former store manager and WUDC Councillor, he took a great interest in the affairs of the club and was an official for many years. Honorary president of the Over Sixties was Victor Dillon a local builder and chairman of Sunniside Social Club.

A military tattoo at Ravensworth Castle in 1936. Saxons built the beginnings of the original castle but after the Norman Conquest a succession of Norman barons ruled there till 1367. In 1607 the surroundings were bought by Thomas Liddell, a wealthy merchant and coal owner from Newcastle, and this was the beginning of the Liddells of Ravensworth. The third, Thomas Liddell, became a Baron after he helped hold Newcastle against the Scots, by 1747 this became an Earldom. The family produced many worthy citizens, some of them scholars. One of whom was Henry George, he became Dean of Christchurch and Oxford. He had a daughter, Alice, who was thought to be the inspiration behind the book *Alice in Wonderland* written by his curate, Charles Lutwidge Dodgson (Lewis Carroll). At the end of the 18th century, the castle was developed on a grand scale and gradually replaced the old fortress. Designed by John Nash, its beautiful grounds and woods were spectacularly beautiful. The Liddells held the estate until 1919 when they decided to leave for their country estate at Eslington Park. In 1978 the Lord Ravensworth of that time sold the estate to the tenants and the resident farmer. Unfortunately due to subsidence caused by the coal owners extracting coal from under the castle, the building collapsed into ruin. Large sections of it are still visible, largely overgrown but still strangely majestic, parts of it towering over the trees.

The People's History

To receive a catalogue of our latest titles send a large SAE to:

The People's History
Suite 1, Byron House
Seaham Grange Business Park, Seaham
County Durham, SR7 0PY

www.peopleshistory.co.uk